FOLLOWING JESUS EVERY DAY

CHRISTOPH CARDINAL SCHÖNBORN

FOLLOWING JESUS EVERY DAY

How Believing Transforms Living

Edited by Hubert Philipp Weber

Translated by Brian McNeil

IGNATIUS PRESS   SAN FRANCISCO

CONTENTS

EDITOR'S INTRODUCTION

On one Sunday evening each month, the archbishop of Vienna, Christoph Cardinal Schönborn, holds a catechesis in Saint Stephen's Cathedral on central themes of the faith. In the church year 2001–2002, he dedicated a series of these addresses to the basic questions of Christian morality. The talks were recorded, and the texts were transcribed and photocopied. In order to make the catecheses available to a wider reading public, the editor has revised these transcripts. After the publication of the book *Jesus als Christus erkennen* (To know Jesus as the Christ) by Herder in 2002, a second volume now presents further impulses for the deepening of one's faith.

"Preach the word, be urgent in season and out of season" (2 Tim 4:2). This exhortation to Bishop Timothy is particularly relevant today, when it is a question of preaching Christian morality. This is no easy matter. There is a great temptation to "moralize", to insist on merely obeying the rules—or else to seek to retain the favor of one's hearers by avoiding the more demanding questions and emphasizing above all the subjective aspects of moral insight. The path that Cardinal Schönborn takes here endeavors to avoid both extremes.

"Catechesis" means a strengthening in the faith. Accordingly, a catechesis on the foundations of morality is meant to strengthen the believing hearers in their Christian conduct and in the awareness that they, as moral beings, bear responsibility and are always at risk of falling into sin. But Cardinal Schönborn also continually points out that we are not left alone in our conduct, in the difficult task of coping with life's challenges: God's grace helps us, since it is present in the human person from the outset, as a gift that God invites us to grasp. Thanks to this divine help, good conduct is possible, as we see in the great examples of the saints. Thus, this cycle of catechesis leads from the basic question—What is ethical conduct, and how is it possible?—to the question of holiness.

These talks have various sources, each of which makes its own contribution. The reflections on morality always begin with human experience. Morality belongs inseparably to human existence.

What then is the specific character of *Christian* morality? Why do we Christians consider the fact that we give a specific orientation to the conduct of our lives to be an essential element of our faith? Here the general human experience of life is enriched by another factor.

Human beings bear the marks of sin. What this means for us is fully revealed when we know that Jesus Christ has redeemed us. In other words, the Christian faith enlarges our awareness of sin. The first source of the faith is sacred Scripture, with which the tradition and the teaching of the Church are closely linked. Some of the theologians of the first millennium, the Church Fathers, are quoted here, and Saint Thomas Aquinas, the most famous teacher of the Western Church, has a special place in these catecheses. (Like Cardinal Schönborn, he too belonged to the Dominican order.) The liturgy and its texts are also important. When the catecheses address the Church's teaching, they find their principal point of reference in the *Catechism of the Catholic Church*. The main point here is not to gain an external knowledge of the *Catechism* but rather to understand its affirmations as part of the totality of the faith and to find in them guidance for one's own life.

The Church possesses another rich treasury of experience, namely, the countless saints, whose exemplary lives help us to find an orientation today. In the course of two thousand years, they have imitated Christ in their lives in a tremendous variety of historical circumstances. This immense wealth offers us many elements that can enrich our Christian living.

The first catechesis investigates the *foundations*. Every human being bears in himself a sensitivity to the good and a yearning for the goal of life, namely, happiness. All the many commandments and prohibitions that exist in our life are at the service of this longing that is common to us all.

Ethical behavior is possible only where people act in *freedom*. The thirst for freedom is so strong that many risk their lives to attain this immeasurable good. But how do we deal with our freedom? When does freedom reach its highest point?

The third catechesis speaks of the *conscience*. There is always a risk that freedom may lead us astray if the inner compass of the conscience is lacking or if we do not pay attention to it. The question of the formation of the conscience and of our personal attitude is also important. This catechesis was held two months after the terrible attacks of September 11, 2001. What are we to say about the conscience of the terrorists? Naturally, the hero of the Christian conscience is a different figure altogether: not the fanatic, but the saint.

Freedom does not entitle us to do whatever comes into our heads. Freedom is closely linked to *responsibility*. Human conduct is moral because the human person himself can direct his actions and must therefore also accept the consequences of what he does. God gives us freedom but also

responsibility. This is why we must also bear the consequences of our actions.

The fifth catechesis takes up a classic theme that is sometimes neglected in modern discussions: the *passions*. These are
an element in human life. Many saints were passionate people—and their emotions helped make their lives exemplary.
Jesus too encounters us in the Gospels with his passions.

After this, the sixth catechesis speaks of the *virtues*. This
word is no longer fashionable, but both the concept and the
matter to which it refers were already familiar to the ancient
Greek philosophers. The doctrine of the virtues tells us how
we can change our lives in the direction of the good, in small
and larger steps.

God does not leave us to our own devices when we act. The
Christian is led along the path to God with the *gifts of the Holy
Spirit*. Every Christian can identify times in his life when he has
experienced the Spirit. But do we trust the Spirit to lead us? Are
we open to the working of the Spirit?

A catechesis about Christian morality would be incom-
plete if it did not speak of *sin*. The point here is not to depress
people, still less to make them ill, by a continuous emphasis
on their sinfulness. Whenever the Christian faith speaks of
sin, it does so in the context of redemption. Only the one
whom Christ has set free knows the real gravity and weight
of sin.

The ninth catechesis speaks of *grace*. This word, which we
read so often in the writings of the apostle Paul, seems to
have become merely a specialized theological term, almost
devoid of relevance to real life. But when we look more
closely, we discover that something of decisive importance
for our lives is involved here. Everything is God's gift. When
we speak of grace, this is the central message.

The final catechesis takes up this point and speaks of *justification and holiness* as the realization of grace in the human person. All are called to take the hand of God, so that he can free them from their sins and make them new persons. All are called to become holy. This catechesis was held on June 16, 2002, the day on which Pope John Paul II canonized Saint Pius of Pietrelcina, "Padre Pio". The example of this saint illustrates the meaning of holiness and the path that leads to this goal.

Hubert Philipp Weber

I

"CHRISTIAN, RECOGNIZE YOUR DIGNITY!"

The Basis of Christian Morality

God of mercy, come to meet our action and reflection with your grace and accompany it, so that everything we begin may have its beginning with you and may be completed with your help. We make our prayer through Christ our Lord. Amen.

You Must!—You Must Not!

Let us begin with the word "morality". It has negative overtones for many people because it evokes prohibitions and commandments: "You must not ...!" and "You must ...!" And it is indeed true that much of our morality is concerned with prohibitions and commandments. When we speak of moral driving, we mean correct behavior on the roads. When we speak of public morality, this has a lot to do with "You must ...!" and "You must not ...!" You must pay your taxes; you must not evade paying them! You must observe the traffic regulations; you must not disobey them! In virtually every sphere of life, some things are prohibited, while others are enjoined upon us. All this belongs to a wide-ranging sphere of rules we must obey if life is to be tolerable at all. This is a fact we simply have to accept—and much of this involves compulsion. We would probably pay no taxes, or only very little, if we did not know that we would be punished if we failed to pay them. Some of us would probably drive faster than the speed limit, if we did not know [the possible consequences]. The same is true of drinking and driving. Fear of potential sanctions is an important means of keeping us within the realm of the decent and appropriate conduct necessary for life in society. A great deal of public morality is concerned with the observation of requirements that are laid down in advance. Where there are no such rules, life in society soon becomes a torture.

I remember my visit to Pedro Carbo, a city with forty thousand inhabitants in Ecuador, where two of the priests from our diocese are working. The citizens drove out the police because they were so corrupt that people understandably thought they would have a better life without these policemen than with them. The consequence is that theft and murder have become everyday events. Whoever can get hold of a gun has one, in order to defend himself. It is a tremendous privilege to live in a country where it is safe to walk on the streets!

A lot of morality concerns obligations: "You must!" and "You must not!" Our own experience or observation teaches us that both children and adults can learn a lot in this way. Often enough, it is the protective walls of prohibitions and commandments that protect us from doing something stupid, guarding us against dangers from both within and outside ourselves. We easily let ourselves be carried away by the passions, and it is important to have boundary markers that show us where the limits are. This, however, explains why the word "morality" has negative overtones: it seems like something that restricts us, a corset that deprives us of our freedom of movement. The word "morality" often sounds far removed from pleasure and joy.

The Path to a Good Life

After this initial look at the word "morality", we may well ask: Do we do what is good only because we are compelled to do so, because ultimately we have no other choice than to behave at least in a fairly respectable manner? Do we avoid evil only because we are afraid of the negative consequences—the penalties and sanctions? Doubtless, this will often be the case. We are human beings who know that we also incline toward evil; in the language of our faith, we say that we are *marked by original sin*. This is why we need these boundaries that prevent us from making mistakes. Fear of the consequences of wrong conduct has kept many people from doing something bad and helped them to do something good; and this applies to us too. Often, we do what is good simply because it is required of us: we must behave in an appropriate manner. The stewardess on a plane must be friendly—otherwise, she will lose her job. She is not asked if she "feels like" being friendly to the passengers, or whether she enjoys smiling. She is obliged to do so. An unfriendly stewardess will soon be out of work. At first glance, therefore, it seems as if the primary factor in morality would be this external framework, where we must do some things and must avoid doing others. A closer look suggests that there is more to it than that. It is perfectly possible that the stewardess is genuinely friendly, and she is smiling not only because her job requires this. Perhaps she smiles because she enjoys doing

so, because she sees this as something positive. And this helps
her to overcome herself on days when she is in a bad mood,
so that even then she manages to be friendly.

What are we saying when we say that someone is kind?
Do we mean someone who is obliged by external compulsion and necessity to be kind, someone who is as it were
forced to do so? Or do we not rather mean that kindness
shines forth from within, from his eyes, his heart, his whole
being? We call someone a genuinely kind person only when
kindness has an interior aspect, when it is a characteristic of
his life. When we meet someone like that, we feel an echo
in our own selves: it is quite simply good for us to be in the
company of kind persons, just as it can be very strenuous to
be in the company of those in a bad mood (to say nothing of
those who are embittered). We spontaneously find it more
humane when someone's kindness comes from within, not as
the result of exterior coercion; when a smile comes from the
heart, not from a mask that one's professional work obliges
one to assume. We have all met people like that, and they
inspire in us the wish to live like them. We sense that this
has something to do with a successful life. Such a person is
perhaps more of a human being than I find myself to be—I
see myself vacillating from one mood to another, and I would
like to be like that person. Something in me looks for a path
that will permit me to be kind because my heart wants this,
not merely because I am forced to be so.

This, however, is accompanied by the sobering insight
that this is not automatic. Naturally, there are people with
a more cheerful temperament, who find it easier than others
to be kind. One who has a gloomy temperament will find
it more arduous to be kind than one naturally inclined to
kindness. But we notice that such an endeavor is possible:
I can work to make my life more human. Clearly, this does

not succeed all by itself. It is rather easier for animals, since these things are innate. A newborn kitten does not need to learn very much from its mother: it crawls off at once and is very soon independent. It does not have to learn how to become a cat, since this is programmed: its conduct is guided by its instincts. We could say the kitten learns without any effort how to be a cat. Things are different with us. Successful human existence is not acquired without effort. From the first instant of our lives, we are dependent on receiving an enormous quantity of help. A child who is abandoned cannot survive. We look at a newborn child in a very different way from a kitten or a puppy. We ask: What will become of you? What will your life be like? Will it succeed or not? What will you make of yourself? What will others make of you? Will you be a good person?

All these questions are present when a child is brought for baptism. Perhaps this is why many who themselves are no longer practicing members of the Church nevertheless bring their children to be baptized. They know that they cannot take it for granted that the life of their child will succeed: What paths will you take? What will happen to you in the course of your life? And they ask: What will you make of the things that happen to you? How will you cope with happiness and unhappiness? Adolf Hitler was once a newborn child like this; so was Mother Teresa.

Was it simply fate that decreed that Hitler's life took one direction and Mother Teresa's another?
Was it already written in the stars?
Why are we horrified by the course of the one life and so grateful for the course of the other life?
Why is our heart warmed by the thought of Mother Teresa?
Why do we regard her life as successful?

Why do we regard that other life as a mistaken path, as the terrible failure of a human path through life?

What Is Happiness?

This brings us to the primary human question: What constitutes a successful life? What does "success" mean here?

What is the "successful" element in such a life? Aristotle, the great Greek philosopher, says that we want to be happy.[1] I believe that it is difficult to argue against this proposition. Everyone wants to be happy, or (if he is unhappy) to become happy. And we want to remain happy. We want our happiness to last. No one willingly makes his home in unhappiness.

How then can I become happy? This is the great question to which morality is asked to offer an answer, and this brings us to a great controversy among those who have written on this subject: Is the moral life concerned about happiness or about duty? Must I do what is good, or am I allowed to look for happiness? I recall here an American lady, now dead, whose grandmother had compelled her to learn to play the piano. She hated this, as is often the case with children when they are obliged to learn a musical instrument. At the age of fourteen, however, she began to enjoy it, and then her grandmother, who was a strict puritan, forbade her to play the piano, since one does not do anything that gives enjoyment! What is the correct measure of the ethical quality of an action: duty or happiness? We will return to this question repeatedly, and we shall see that there is no antithesis here.

The ancient pagan and Christian masters say that happiness is a criterion for the good life. The great question is this:

---

[1] Aristotle, *Nicomachean Ethics* 1095a.

What is true happiness? In what does it consist? Many things are enjoyable and entertaining at the moment; they may even bring us joy. But after some time has passed, we notice that this was not yet real happiness. We enjoy acknowledgment and honor, but with time we notice that happiness cannot consist in receiving honors and testimonials. Many people seek happiness in wealth; and life is certainly better in many ways when one has material security than when one lacks this. And yet we know how quickly wealth can disappear. It is profoundly true to state that happiness cannot lie in money alone. This is why both the philosophy of the early masters and Christian philosophy return again and again to this question: What makes us really happy?

It is certain that everyone aims at happiness, as a very simple example shows: look at advertising! No one would try to advertise an article by saying: "This will make you unhappy." A book by the well-known American advertising expert Ernest Dichter has the title *The Strategy of Desire*.[2] When advertisers sing the praises of something—it may be cigarettes, underwear, soap powder, a life insurance policy, a lottery ticket, or even religious instruction in school (which can certainly do with a bit of advertising)—they always aim to convince the one who sees their advertisement (i.e., the consumer) that the one who buys this product is buying happiness. The advertisement aims at directing people's wishes to what it wants to sell. People want to be happy, and the art of a good advertisement is to direct this longing for happiness to the object it wants to sell, and to demonstrate that this object promises happiness. Everyone strives for happiness. But this striving encounters many hindrances—a lack of money (if you believe that money makes you happy), a lack of power, a lack of success. And

[2] Garden City, NY: Doubleday, 1960.

morality too seems to keep on erecting barriers that say: "You must not do this! You ought not to do that!" It seems as if morality does a lot to thwart us in our search for happiness. That is what children often feel when their parents tell them what they are to do or their teachers demand that they learn something. That does not look like happiness!

Surely we have to put the question differently: What makes us happy? What kind of happiness lasts—not something I will be sorry about tomorrow but a happiness that fills my life and passes the final test: a happiness that not even death can destroy? We all know by experience that not everything that is pleasant makes us truly happy. This does not mean that pleasure is forbidden; but we know that lasting happiness also (not: *only!*) involves sacrifice, struggle, and suffering. When we speak of a happy marriage, we certainly do not mean a marriage in which all is pleasure. Happiness has its price, but it is possible. Happy marriages do exist. This does not in the least mean that it is simple to lead that kind of married life.

As Christians, we believe that the longing in our hearts for happiness, this longing with which we are born, is ultimately not in vain. We believe that God has planted this longing for happiness in the human heart not out of sadism or out of wickedness as in the myth of Sisyphus, who keeps on having to roll a stone upward—but when he reaches the top, the stone rolls back down to the ground. No, God did not plant this longing for happiness in our heart in order to torment us with a futile striving.

Signposts to a Successful Life

As a child and a teenager, I heard many sermons by our parish priest, but I must admit that I do not remember many of them. We loved our priest, and I remember well the feeling that radiated from him when he stood high up in the pulpit, the benevolence and love that flowed down upon us. I remember only one single sentence, a rock that stands out from the stream of forgetfulness: "God wants us to be happy." I noted this sentence—but why precisely this one?

"See, I have set before you this day life and good, death and evil.... I have set before you life and death, blessing and curse; therefore choose life, that you and your descendants may live" (Deut 30:15, 19). These words come right at the end of the fifth book of Moses, where God once again presents his people with the alternatives: life and death, happiness and unhappiness. Choose life! Choose happiness! With these words, God is also telling his people: We must choose. We must make a decision, and whether we harvest happiness or unhappiness, life or death, depends on making the correct choice.

In the next catecheses, we will look at the following questions: How do I choose life? How does this happen step-by-step along my path in life? Biblical, Jewish, and Christian morality sees itself as providing directives for a happy life. God wants us to be happy. So that we can find this path and take it, God gives us help in the form of signposts. We will return again and again to these signposts. The most important are the following:

Commandments

God indicates the path to us by means of his *commandments*. This word, like the word "prohibition", now takes on a different note: God is showing us the way to happiness. God does not want to cut us off from happiness through prohibitions and commandments; on the contrary, he says to us: Take this path, or avoid that path, because this path leads to happiness and that path leads to unhappiness. God tells the

people of Israel: "If you obey the commandments of the
LORD your God which I command you this day, by loving
the LORD your God, by walking in his ways, and by keeping
his commandments and his statutes and his ordinances, then
you shall live" (Deut 30:16). Similarly, when the rich young
man asks Jesus: "Teacher, what good deed must I do, to have
eternal life?" Jesus replies: "If you would enter life, keep the
commandments" (Mt 19:16–17). Accordingly, we will have
to examine more closely how it is that the commandments
of God are a path to happiness. Because God desires our happiness, he shows the way that leads to happiness and warns
against taking the path that leads to unhappiness.

Conscience

We will speak not only of these external signposts—the commandments—but also of an internal compass. God has put a
compass in our hearts, which functions with great precision
but continually needs to be adjusted and fine-tuned. We call
this compass, which leads us in the direction of happiness,
the *conscience*. This is the inner signpost to happiness. When
we have pangs of conscience, the message is this: Do not take
this particular path, for it is not good. When our conscience
reproaches us after we have done something bad, it is saying:
The path you took was not a good path.

Models

In addition to these two signposts, the external signpost of the
commandments and the internal signpost of the conscience,
God has given us *models* to help us on our path. These are
people who show us what it means to take a good path and
who reveal what a successful life is. Precisely in the sphere of

our conduct, models play a very decisive role: they teach us how to live. This is why the ethical teacher is himself a part of his ethical teaching—and there is no ethical teacher greater than Jesus.

Reality

There is a fourth gift God gives us to help us find the path to happiness, and this may perhaps sound surprising: *reality* is a great teacher. It compels us to be realistic and sober and not let ourselves get distracted. We know that we cannot live as if reality did not exist. If I eat too much in the evening because I enjoy my food too much, I cannot escape the nocturnal reality that takes the form of nightmares and sleeplessness. Reality catches up with us and tells us where we took a wrong step. Sins against the environment bring their own penalty: they show that our behavior inflicts violence on the environment and often causes long-lasting harm. We ourselves suffer the consequences, which show what we did wrong. The reality of your own body will catch up with you if you do not keep to the right measure in eating, drinking, and enjoyment. Abuse of the body leads to illness, the damage to one's health that reminds us what healthy living means.

This is true in every area of life. Reality informs us whether we are taking the right path. Injustices great and small can go unnoticed for a time, but sooner or later they rebound on us. Untruthfulness can be successful for the moment, but as an eloquent German proverb says: "Lies have short legs." Truth and reality belong together. If we deny reality in our words and deeds, reality strikes back.

I have spoken here of *reality*. Traditional philosophy and ethics call this "nature". Ethically good behavior is behavior in accordance with nature, not something contrary to nature.

It keeps to the ordering of things, to the nature of the human person, and to the nature of the environment. The slogan "Act naturally" will remind the older ones among us of a Beatles song that was popular when I was young: "Act naturally!" But what is in keeping with human nature? What is natural for us? Is monogamy natural? (Polygamy exists in many cultures.) Is homosexuality "unnatural"? (Many say it is merely one variant among others.) What is natural? We are confronted today by great questions in bioethics: Is cloning contrary to nature? Is the manipulation of the genetic code contrary to human nature? But why then should an operation for appendicitis not be "contrary to human nature"? We see here (and we will encounter many more examples) how difficult it is in a specific individual judgment to say what is in keeping with nature and what is contrary to it. This is certainly connected with the nature of ethical conduct itself: the general principles are clear, but the more we come down to praxis, the more difficult it sometimes is to make the correct judgment in individual cases.

Everyone who thinks in genuinely human terms will agree that one must do what is good and avoid what is evil. But what does this mean—to take a very concrete example—when we fight against terrorism in today's situation? If we give in to the terrorists' demands, may this perhaps encourage them, so that the terror will become even worse? If we react with the use of force, does this risk intensifying the terror and provoking new actions? What is the correct decision in this specific situation? This reminds us how urgent it is that we pray for the politicians who must make such decisions. We also must do what is good and avoid what is evil: we are all agreed on this.

In the Old Testament, there are 661 commandments. Since life is so varied, the people of Israel attempted to listen to the will of God and to lay down many individual regulations so that they could respond to as many different situations as possible: What must be done in these specific circumstances? What is God's will here and now? Everyone can grasp that we should act in keeping with our nature and in a way appropriate to reality. This should prompt us to reflect: Is it right to use up fossil fuels in our automobiles and planes to such an extent that they will be depleted a few decades from now? Are we not doing something here that is contrary to nature?

Even if someone is clearly a model for us, we cannot simply translate that person's life into our own. Mother Teresa may truly be an exemplary figure, but I cannot live her life. I must live my own life, recognizing my own talents and carrying out the tasks that are mine. I must discover and put into practice the will of God in my life. Models can help me here—they can stimulate me and encourage me—but I cannot delegate my life to them. I myself must make the right decisions. It is often difficult for parents when they have to accept letting go of their children because, in the last analysis, no matter how much the parents may be an example to their children, and no matter how many precepts they may pass on, the children have to find their own way in life.

Morality and Christian Morality

The yearning for happiness is written on our hearts. Our task, so to speak, is to take the path to a successful and happy life; but first we have to seek this path. We want to be (or become) happy, and we are certainly allowed to do so! But it is not always easy to find the correct path. It is painful when we take wrong paths; but although God gives us the freedom to take such paths, he nevertheless gives us points of orientation. I mention four of these.

First, the commandment of God is a light on our path, because we cannot see the goal clearly without this help: "Keep the commandments, and you will live!" (see Mt 19:17; Deut 30:16).

Second, the conscience functions as a compass that tells me when I am leaving the right path.

Third, reality—our human nature and the world in which we live—demands that we behave appropriately.

Fourth, there are models who show us that a successful life is possible and who encourage us to believe that this is genuinely available to us too, even if we have still to discover the true life and take hold of it.

This will be our great theme: following these points of orientation.

I wish now to ask another question: Is what I have said up to this point Christian morality? Is it not basically something that every human being receives as help toward a genuinely human life? Is there in fact a *Christian* morality? Ought we not rather to say that it would be good if we Christians observed *human* morality? There is nothing wrong about being respectable persons! Does Christianity add anything to this? The subtitle of this catechesis is "The Basis of Christian Morality". The third section of the *Catechism of the Catholic Church*, which deals with morality, has the title "Life in Christ". So it is clear that another dimension exists. This section begins with a quotation from a Christmas sermon of Pope Leo the Great (d. 461). I would like to call this the "fifth dimension", which goes beyond the realm of natural ethics:

> Christian, recognize your dignity and, now that you share in God's own nature, do not return to your former base condition by sinning. Remember who is your head and of whose

body you are a member. Never forget that you have been rescued from the power of darkness and brought into the light of the Kingdom of God.[3]

Christian ethics is a life in Christ, a life with Christ. The *Catechism* goes on to show in detail that something new is involved here.

I should like to conclude with a few words on each of the first four dimensions. For the Christian, God's *commandments* are not merely external precepts. The Holy Spirit writes them on our hearts, and love in our hearts tells us what the commandments mean. They are not imposed from outside us. Everyone has a *conscience*. But the Holy Spirit gives the Christian conscience something extra, namely, his guidance, his gifts, and ultimately his love. For the Christian, "Act naturally!" also means "Act supernaturally!", that is, act in a way that goes beyond nature. And this means faith, hope, and love. Finally, it is the Lord himself who is our *model*. Christ shows us a higher path that surpasses all our own endeavors to behave morally. I intend to reflect on this path in the following catecheses, and I hope that we will be able to make at least a little progress along this path.

[3] *Sermon* 21, 2–3; *Catechism of the Catholic Church*, 2nd ed. (Vatican City: Libreria Editrice Vaticana / Washington, D.C.: United States Catholic Conference, 2000), 1691 (hereafter cited as *CCC*).

2

TRUE FREEDOM IN CHRIST

Almighty and merciful God, keep far away from us whatever is dangerous, and take away whatever oppresses us in body and soul, so that we may do your will with a free heart. We make our prayer through Christ our Lord. Amen.

Once I spoke in Rome with Vietnamese boat people who told me the story of their escape from communist Vietnam. They put out to sea in a boat, facing all kinds of dangers, in the hope that they could somehow get out of this communist country, which was one huge prison. Listening to their story made me aware of how immensely strong the urge to find freedom is. Think of all the trouble they took: building a boat secretly for weeks or even months, equipping it at terrible risk if they were found out, and then setting off on a journey beset by the threat of being caught by the coast guard or meeting pirates—to say nothing of the nagging uncertainty about whether they would ever make it through storms and perils to freedom. Freedom is truly precious! In another time and place hope was kindled in many people when their ships entered the harbor in New York and they saw the Statue of Liberty. This meant that their dream had come true: they were free at last!

Freedom—Something Immensely Precious

What is freedom? Freedom is what makes morality possible. If I cannot decide freely to do something, I am not responsible for what I do, and I cannot be called to account for it. If a dog bites someone, we do not take it to court; but if its owner omitted to muzzle it, then he can certainly face legal proceedings. The dog is not responsible for what it does, since it acts instinctively. This is why its conduct is neither good nor bad, even when we are told that some dogs are particularly bad and that others have a sweet nature, or that animals have a good or bad character. An aggressive dog will not be allowed to roam around freely; but dogs are not thrown into prison!

There have been endless discussions about freedom down through the history of philosophy. Does it exist? Or does it not exist? Where are its boundaries? What are its preconditions?

And yet, if we look around us in ordinary human life, we see that freedom is always assumed to exist, without any great reflections on the theoretical problems involved. We are called to account all the time for what we do or fail to do. We expect all the time that the people with whom we have dealings will behave responsibly, and they expect the same of us.

I often think, as I drive along the highway at eighty miles an hour: How is it that we assume that everyone else will behave responsibly in this situation? You pass a truck at eighty miles an hour, and the truck keeps to its own part of the road because its driver behaves responsibly. Otherwise, a catastrophe occurs. We hear every day of such catastrophes, with phrases such as "human error", "excessive speed", "drunk driving", or simply "carelessness". Subsequently, in painstaking legal investigations, the questions of guilt and responsibility require the judge to determine how much guilt attaches to the person who caused the accident: To what extent can we speak of blame here? In everyday life, we take it for granted that people will behave responsibly. If the accident is caused by a defect in the automobile, no one will be blamed for what happened, unless we discover that someone in the garage neglected to do his job properly: here, it is not the driver of the car but the mechanic who bears the blame for the accident. We are all familiar with this concept of responsibility and of a greater or lesser degree of guilt. If someone deliberately or carelessly puts another person at risk, we view this more seriously than a situation where someone unintentionally puts another at risk or causes an accident. This means that harsher penalties are exacted when someone drives without any consideration for others on the road than when someone falls asleep at the wheel for a couple of seconds and thereby causes an accident. (In the latter case, however, this driver is certainly guilty if he failed to take the necessary precautions that would have prevented him from falling asleep.) A good friend of mine suffered a stroke while driving, and the result was an accident in which a person died. But neither he nor anyone else was to blame for this accident; as the insurance companies say, it was an "act of God".

We are rightly outraged when children are sexually abused. We know the profound and terrible scars this can leave on their psyche for the rest of their lives. It is not by chance that Jesus spoke so sternly to those who give offense to "these little ones": "It would be better for him to have a great millstone fastened round his neck and to be drowned in the depth of the sea" (Mt 18:6). These are terrible words. A man who has pedophilic temptations might perhaps say that he cannot resist or dominate his urges, that these are stronger than he is, and that he is not free at such moments. No doubt, we would not wish to be unduly harsh with people who give way to their weaknesses, since we all know how weak we human beings are; nevertheless, the pedophile will be told in court that he ought to have avoided the danger. He ought to have gone to therapy. He ought to have done something, for it was his duty to ensure that he was not the passive plaything of his own urges. In short, he is responsible for what he does. He is also responsible for establishing the correct structures for his own life, especially if he has a position of trust as educator, teacher, or priest.

Here I am deliberately prescinding from the question of sin, in other words, of guilt in the eyes of God; we shall return to this later, in chapter 8. Here we are speaking of freedom. What does it mean to bear responsibility, to live daily with responsibility, and to be called to account even in situations where we do not perceive our responsibility? All this presupposes that we are in fact free. Philosophy can reflect on the true nature of freedom as much as it likes; in our everyday lives, freedom is taken for granted. Freedom exists, and we bear responsibility, since we are human beings, not animals. But do we not often experience our freedom, and the obligations that are linked to it, as fetters with which we are obliged to live—more out of compulsion than out of a genuine freedom?

The True Criterion of Freedom

Before we inquire further into the nature of freedom, it will be helpful to recall that we ought to be a lot more astonished than we are at the realities of our everyday life, since we certainly cannot take them for granted. They help us to approach this difficult question of freedom with an attitude of astonishment at the fact that freedom exists; at the same time, the realities of everyday life keep our feet firmly planted on the ground. When I attempt to analyze the prevalent attitudes toward freedom today, I have the impression of a profound divergence, indeed almost a contradiction, between the positions people take. On the one side, we find an *under-estimation* of freedom, and on the other hand an *overestimation* of freedom.

Freedom Underestimated

In many ways, freedom is underestimated today. We are conditioned and marked by so many factors. Some people consult their horoscope every morning and want to know what the stars have to say about love and happiness. They believe that our lives are determined by the stars. Saint Thomas Aquinas says very clearly that there is indeed an influence of the constellations on our life, just as nature influences us; but this is a general influence that sets no limitations on our freedom.

Some hold that the human person is genetically programmed in such a way that everything is laid down beforehand in the genetic code that one receives at conception, when ovum and sperm come together. "Genetically programmed" would therefore mean "not free". Others hold that we are totally influenced by our environment, on which we are necessarily dependent. Others again hold that we are largely determined by our instincts and that there is no space left for freedom. Let me mention one example that is much discussed at present. There is a lobby in support of homosexuality that maintains that homosexuality is genetically programmed: it is not a matter of one's own choice but something determined from the outset. Scientists disagree about whether external influences or genetic predispositions play a larger role in the genesis of homosexuality; but even if the latter were the case, the question would remain: How does the person deal with this tendency? If something is innate, is one nevertheless free to decide how one's life is to be structured? This applies not only to the question of homosexuality but to every sphere of life. Do we have the freedom to impose a structure on our innate qualities, or are we completely programmed in advance by genes, instincts, dispositions, our environment, or the stars?

We are frequently told that thinking is a product of the brain. Scientists are quoted as saying that the intellect and freedom are products of the brain. One can of course reply at once by asking: Is this hypothesis, or the article in which it is formulated, merely the product of chemical processes in the brain—or did someone actually think it up? The great Jewish philosopher Hans Jonas (d. 1993), a prominent champion of human freedom and responsibility, once told the following story. In the nineteenth century, three natural scientists who were later to become famous—Ernst von Brücke, Emil du Bois-Reymond, and Hermann von Helmholtz—got together and took a vow that for the rest of their lives, they would admit only a strictly materialistic explanation of the human person. Everything is matter; spirit does not exist. Hans Jonas rightly points out that this vow that the three scientists took was an act of the intellect. They committed themselves to remain faithful to this promise as long as they lived. But this must mean that they were free. And that cannot just be the product of matter.

Are all the tremendous discoveries and achievements of science merely the product of a prior genetic determination or of material processes? What then are we to say of the scientists' responsibility? Is this too something programmed in advance? Was it already determined that the atom would be discovered, then the splitting of the atom, and then the utilization of this splitting to make an atomic bomb? Was the discovery of bacterial weapons determined beforehand? Is the possibility to use great discoveries well or badly merely the chemical product of our brain? Or is it guided by the human intellect, so that we can genuinely speak of responsibility? In short, the question is whether responsibility does in fact exist. At a very early date in the modern period, we already see this remarkable tendency to deny human freedom. Basically, this is a new form of the fatalism found in the pagans of old—with the difference that now it is not the gods but our genes that determine everything. According to this view, the human person is a programmed machine. The program may indeed be very complex, but much of it has been deciphered by now. And here we must ask once again: Was it the brain alone that deciphered the genetic code, or was this the work of human researchers driven by a thirst for knowledge, with all the responsibility this implies?

Freedom Overestimated

On the other side, we find the tendency to overestimate freedom. Thinkers in the modern period have always been tempted to understand freedom as something free of all ties. Freedom thus means: I am the one I myself want to be. I make myself; I determine myself. I am not tied to any presuppositions. In a certain sense, I am my own creator. This understanding of freedom as unfettered self-realization is very widespread and permeates our everyday lives. "To live without ties": this is the very essence of freedom—to be able to travel to the Maldives if one wants to; to do whatever one wants, without having to observe any prior conditions, without being limited by laws, traditions, or ties—*this* is freedom!

If we look at the history of the West to see where this under-standing of freedom has its roots, we can go as far back as the nominalism that was the dominant intellectual position in Vienna and many other European universities in the late Middle Ages. Here we find the view that freedom means a lack of ties; but since this can also be dangerous, it must be fenced in by laws and regulations that we are compelled to observe, by a whole set of commandments and prohibitions: "You must" and "You must not". And this is experienced as a limitation on the true nature of freedom.

Freedom as a Gift from God

Both these views of freedom, its underestimation ("Basically, the human person is programmed in advance") and its over-estimation ("Basically, the human person is his own creator") have points of contact with our experience. We frequently feel ourselves to be terribly far from freedom, and we are inclined to believe that this must mean a lack of all ties. But let us now look at revelation, where we will find a very dif ferent picture of freedom. What does God tell us about free-dom? What light does Scripture give us?

The Gift of Freedom

The first thing Scripture tells us about freedom is surprising, but faith sees this as wholly natural, since faith sheds a won-derful light on this question: *Freedom is a gift*. It is created by God, and this means that God wants me to be free. He has made us in such a way that we are free. If we reflect on this, we see that it involves a profound mystery. We are all crea-tures, and God has given us everything: our existence, our life, and our freedom. Precisely this is the mystery: I am free, but this freedom makes me dependent. God has given it to me; I have not made myself free. To be a creature means to be dependent, and perhaps our problem today (and through-out the modern period) consists in accepting dependence. We see dependence as the opposite of freedom. But when we read the Bible, we see that we are free precisely when we are dependent on God, as his creatures. Our freedom is not without ties; rather, it is a freedom that we receive as a *task* to be accomplished. Freedom is entrusted to me as something I must shape and take care of.

The Contradiction of Freedom

This entails an important consequence, which at first sight seems incomprehensible. Let me formulate it briefly, almost in the manner of a slogan: The more we bind ourselves, the freer we are. Let me give you an example. All her life, Mother Teresa bound herself completely to the task God had given her, so unreservedly, that the fifty years of her life as foundress of a religious order and mother of the poor made her totally available to serve God and the poor. All she wanted was to live for Christ in the poor. At first sight, it would appear as if this poor woman had no freedom whatsoever in her life. And yet innumerable people who met Mother Teresa saw her as a wonderfully free person. How can this be so?

"God willed that man should be left in the hand of his own counsel"—the Old Testament text says literally: "He left him in the power of his own inclination" (Sir 15:14)—"so that he might of his own accord seek his creator and freely attain his full and blessed perfection by cleaving to him."[1] This seems

[1] *CCC* 1743.

like a contradiction: freedom means cleaving to God in freedom. But does not freedom mean that I can do what I want, that I need not observe any rules laid down in advance, that I can decide freely where I want to go, what I do, what I read, whether I want to watch a film or go for a walk? To cleave to the will of God—does that not mean an obligation, in other words, a lack of freedom? If I must do the will of another, am I not then bound?

At this point, there is an important distinction to be made. I wonder whether we could say that a person who was completely independent—with no spouse, no children, no acquaintances, no friends—was truly free. Even if I were completely unfettered, even if I were my own boss, I would still be bound to my own nature. It is quite simply the case that I must sleep and eat—and, more difficult still, I must accept myself. I cannot say: "I will take a holiday from myself—I want to be free of myself!" I have to live with myself for the whole of my life; I have to accept that my hair is thinning, that I was born in Bohemia rather than in Hawaii, that I was born in 1945 rather than in 1845, that I am man rather than a woman, that I am I rather than you, and that you are you rather than your neighbor. I am not free to be myself; I must accept this. I am free only to say yes to myself, and that is often hard enough: yes to the life I actually have to lead, yes to the character I actually have, yes to what I have become (and cannot simply alter). I am not free to turn myself into someone else. And yet faith tells us: "For freedom Christ has set us free" (Gal 5:1).

What is freedom? Is it the insight into necessity? That is how the philosopher G. W. F. Hegel defined it. "Insight into necessity" means insight into what I must accept, because no other choice is in fact possible. I must accept, with patience or with anger, with resignation or with fury, that I am dependent on God, on other persons, and on myself. This would mean that I can bear heroically the fact that I am not really free.

Our great models, the saints, show us something else. In them, we see the traces of a freedom greater than we had ever imagined, the freedom for which Christ has set us free. The *Catechism* says: "Freedom is the power to act or not to act, and so to perform deliberate acts of one's own. Freedom attains perfection in its acts when directed toward God, the sovereign Good."[2]

The greater my gift of myself to God and to his will, the greater my freedom. This is the heart of the biblical message. Jesus' entire life was oriented to the Father and to his will: "My food is to do the will of him who sent me" (Jn 4:34). I invite you to join me in pondering this mystery: How is Jesus so independent and free, although he is completely dependent on the Father? We must surely say: He is so independent and free, not "although", but *because* he is completely dependent on the Father.

This brings us to the difficulty that lies deepest in our hearts when we think about freedom, namely, the suspicion that I will renounce my freedom if I obey God, the suspicion that God does not really want me to be free. This suspicion is one of the fruits of the fall. But the experience of the saints says something different: we become free when we trust God and his will and allow ourselves to be led completely by him. Look at Saint John Bosco. Can one imagine a more spontaneous, cheerful, or free person than Don Bosco? But what was the source of this freedom? It grew out of his total orientation to the will of the Father, because God gives us a share in his own divine freedom. And his freedom is

[2] *CCC* 1744.

endlessly creative and inventive. We see the same principle in Francis of Assisi, whose freedom grew out of his obedience to the Father and his love for Christ.

Freedom to Do What Is Good

We are able to choose. "Freedom", as the *Catechism* says, "is the power to act or not to act, and so to perform deliberate acts of one's own." This means that we are able to do good or evil. When I come into my office or my workplace on Monday morning, I can be friendly or ill-tempered: I am free to be either of these. Naturally, it may be harder to be friendly on Monday than on Tuesday, but no one actually forces me to be in a bad mood; I can overcome myself. And it is certainly better for others and for me when I am friendly. This choice is not simply the kind of decision I make when I buy one kind of coffee rather than another, or choose between a blue and a green pullover. The choice to be friendly or ill-tempered is of another character, because *this* choice is between good and evil. These two possibilities that lie before me are not equal in value, and they have different implications for my freedom.

The *Catechism* affirms: "The more one does what is good, the freer one becomes. There is no true freedom except in the service of what is good and just. The choice to disobey and do evil is an abuse of freedom and leads to 'the slavery of sin.' "[3] These words tell us plainly that freedom is not affected when I make a choice between things of equal value and decide to buy one brand rather than another. But freedom is very much affected when the choice lies between good and

[3] *CCC* 1733. Cf. Rom 6:17.

evil. I am free to make evil decisions, but they strip me of my freedom. They hurt others, my own self, and my freedom. In other words, I remain on the path of freedom only when I choose what is good. If I choose what is evil, I have voluntarily set my feet on a path where I cannot be free.

You will get my point if you consider the question: Are we free in heaven? I hope that we will all go to heaven; I pray for this, and I would ask you to pray for one another and for the whole of mankind, that we all may come to heaven. In heaven, we will be happy. Well then: Am I still free to do evil in heaven? Do I still have the freedom of choice between good and evil? In heaven, I am as it were held fast in what is good, because I see God face-to-face. There is no more hesitation, no more deviation from what is good. "We will see God as he is and be like him" forever (cf. 1 Jn 3:2). Will I then lack freedom, if I am in what is good for all eternity? We can no longer make any decision against God when we are in heaven. "As long as freedom has not bound itself definitively to its ultimate good which is God, there is the possibility of *choosing between good and evil*, and thus of growing in perfection or of failing and sinning."[4] Freedom of choice is not yet definitive freedom. As long as it is still possible for me to fall away by choosing what is evil, I am not yet safely established in what is good. As long as I have not yet definitively "lowered my anchor" in God, my freedom is not yet perfect. For as long as I can choose evil, I am in danger; and this danger lurks within all of us.

How about human fidelity? Is this a lack of freedom? When a married couple celebrate their golden wedding anniversary and look back on fifty years of marriage, how

---

[4] *CCC* 1732. Emphasis in all quotations is in the original unless otherwise noted.

do things stand after half a century of fidelity? Do they lack freedom because they remained faithful to one another? But they *want* to remain faithful! And their happiness consists in the fact that, with God's help and with their mutual assistance, they were able to remain faithful. If you ask them, after fifty years: "Would you still say 'I do!' even today?" they will not hesitate for a moment. They will tell you: "I am happy to have been married for fifty years." Do their fifty years of fidelity mean that they are not free? We ought rather to ask about those who (perhaps through a momentary weakness) have taken the path of infidelity: Has this made them freer?

It is perfectly true to say that we are free to sin. But sin does not make us free—that was the promise of the serpent, who was not telling the truth. This is why our freedom stands so much in need of help, in order that it can be realized in the choice of what is good—for our freedom is unstable and at risk. Without the help of other persons and without the help of God, we are helplessly vulnerable to everything that endangers our freedom. On this point, the *Catechism* states:

> The grace of Christ is not in the slightest way a rival of our freedom when this freedom accords with the sense of the true and the good that God has put in the human heart. On the contrary, as Christian experience attests especially in prayer, the more docile we are to the promptings of grace, the more we grow in inner freedom and confidence during trials, such as those we face in the pressures and constraints of the outer world.[5]

Fidelity to God strengthens the good in us. Saint Augustine once prayed: "Lord, save me from myself!" The grace of

[5] CCC 1742.

Christ seeks to strengthen us in our freedom and to protect us from all that endangers it. This is why we believe that we can truly set out on the path of freedom only when Christ takes us by the hand. Christ has called us to freedom, and he has set us free.

3

CONSCIENCE

The Inner Voice That Summons Us to the Good

*Come, Holy Spirit, enlighten our understanding, strengthen
our will, and direct our conscience, so that we may recognize
what is good and have the power to do it. We make our prayer
through Christ our Lord. Amen.*

It seems obvious that each person must follow his conscience;
and yet we ask ourselves whether this is really true. *Must*
each one follow his conscience? Franz Jägerstätter (d. 1943),
a farmer in Upper Austria, followed his conscience when
he resolved to say no to military service under Hitler, even
though he had a wife and three children, and millions of
other men had accepted this obligation. *Must* one always follow one's conscience? After the terrorist attacks in New York
and Washington on September 11, 2001, which displayed
an astonishing degree of technological expertise, a letter by
Mohammed Atta, one of the terrorists, came to light. He
admitted what he had done and claimed that he had prepared
this deed in prayer and had acted out of profound conviction.
Clearly, he was following his conscience. And yet we ask: Is

it not a sign precisely of a lack of conscience to kill thousands of innocent persons merely in order to pursue one's own ideas, no matter how convinced one may be that these ideas are right?

What is the conscience? How do we experience it? What does faith tell us about our conscience? We could call the conscience the compass of ethical living. The question of whether we are acting well or badly has a great deal to do with the question of our conscience.

The Word "Conscience"

Let us begin with the word itself, because language is a finely calibrated instrument that tells us a great deal through the expressions we use. Language registers some things with great sensitivity. The dictionary I consulted includes some examples of how this word is used: "His conscience as a doctor does not permit him to do that." That phrase sounds familiar! Or: "His conscience troubled him." That means that he had to pause for reflection. The dictionary also mentions "a bad conscience" and clarifies what is meant: "a tormenting awareness of having acted wrongly". We are all acquainted with pangs of conscience: I have neglected to do something, I have omitted something I ought to have done, and now my conscience gnaws at me and will give me no peace. The dictionary also speaks of those "without a conscience", in other words, people who "have no sensitivity to the presence of good or evil in what they do". It is a real catastrophe when someone is insensitive to the good and evil in his own conduct; a lack of conscience strikes us as profoundly inhuman.

Accordingly, if we say that someone is without a conscience, we mean that something decisive is lacking in his human existence. "To have something on my conscience" can mean that my conduct was responsible for an accident, or even for someone's death. We also "appeal to someone's conscience", appealing to his sensitivity to what is good, reminding him of his responsibility, and trying to get him to stop behaving wrongly. A "conscientious" person is someone on whom you can rely. Of course, this can be taken to excess: if someone is obsessed by the neurotic idea that he has not acted rightly, or not in exactly the right way, we say that he has "an overscrupulous conscience". If we speak of "a question of conscience", more is involved than a mere technical consideration of ways and means (e.g., "Should we do it in this way, or in that way?"), rather this is a very serious, indeed an existential, question as when Martin Luther said: "Here I stand; I can do no other." In such cases, I must pay due heed to my innermost conviction, and this means that I declare myself ready to accept the consequences, even if these should turn out to be to my own disadvantage.

A "decision made in conscience" means that I have acted out of my innermost conviction. To "force someone's conscience" means that I apply so much pressure that the person finally yields to what I want and acts against his conscience; and we regard such behavior as a very grave offense against the person. The conscience can be "torn" in situations of conflict where we do not really know how to act; this can lead to a "conflict of conscience", if, for example, my professional activity obliges me to do something to which I cannot assent in my conscience. The dictionary I consulted has yet another entry: the "examination of conscience". We are told that this "comes from the vocabulary of the Catholic Church and designates the preparation for sacramental confession". But I would hope that other people too examine their consciences, not only those few Catholics who still go to confession! One last expression: "the formation of the conscience" means ensuring that our conscience remains sensitive and alert.

All this shows how many expressions our language uses to describe the phenomenon of the conscience.

What Is the Origin of the Conscience?

Let me tell you about an event that happened when I was a child; it is not really something I should keep for confession. I may have been about seven or eight years old at the time. There was a carpenter's workshop near our house in the town where we were living, and we often ran past it when we were playing. One day while I was running past this carpenter's workshop, it suddenly occurred to me—I no longer know why—that I could take a plank with me, and so I stole one. It was a little plank, completely unimportant and worthless, but I stole it and ran off with it. When I reached our house, panic seized hold of me: What am I going to do with it now? I hid it on the veranda and was tormented all day by the question: What am I going to do with this plank? Later in the afternoon, I fetched it from the veranda and brought it secretly back to the workshop, replacing it where it had lain before I stole it.

Were my torments that day really connected to my conscience?

What was going on in me?

Was it the fear of discovery, the fear of punishment, or perhaps the fear of disgrace because I had done something that was "not done" and risked being caught red-handed in this profoundly inappropriate conduct?

Let us for the sake of argument say that nothing deeper was involved than such a fear; but even so, we would still have to ask *why* stealing was "not done". Was it merely the fashion in the early 1950s to refrain from stealing?

Was this just an arbitrary rule of behavior in society at that period?

Was it merely the case that one's parents brought one up—or perhaps better, drilled one—to refrain from stealing?

Was the feeling I had unpleasant merely because I had offended against this rule: "One does not do things like that"?

Was the only reason for my fear the fact that I had been brought up in that way?

Or was there also the feeling that we were strangers who had recently settled in that town and that we had to be particularly careful in what we did?

All these considerations add up to one single question: Is the voice of the conscience merely the sum total of the criteria and rules of conduct by which we have been educated, just as animals are trained? We do indeed train our dogs, after all; so, when we train our children, are we aiming to give them a bad conscience when they transgress the rules of their training? Is this comparable to the situation where one feels ill at ease because one is not appropriately dressed, if for example one turns up in jeans at the Viennese Opera Ball? Is anything more involved than the discomfort one feels when one offends the rules for conduct in a particular setting?

Is the conscience the voice that prescribes patterns of behavior that are customary in one particular period of history? People look askance at the one who disobeys such rules, and he himself will feel uneasy. Is this *all* that the famous "pangs of conscience" amount to? Is the conscience nothing more than what the celebrated Viennese psychologist Sigmund Freud called the "superego", something that has been imprinted upon me by my education and hovers over me in the form of compulsion and obligation? According to Freud,

I myself have internalized the superego, and its demands are disclosed in the attitudes that are expected of me (or that I think other people expect of me). Naturally, the conscience is rich in influences of this kind: many factors help shape it, such as our education, the spirit of the age, the context in which we live, our fears and compulsions, our desires and wishes and ideas. *Many voices can be heard in the voice of the conscience*, but how do we discern the voice of the conscience itself in all these voices? Is it audible in this din of voices? What is the contribution of the other voices, and what is the genuine voice of the conscience?

Let us go back to the plank of wood I stole. When I reflect today on what happened then, I am certain that the voice of conscience made itself heard within me, even if a number of other voices were involved too, such as the fear of being discovered. And does not this very fear of discovery itself attest that I did something that per se was not good? As a simple matter of fact, it is not a good thing to steal a plank. And was not this fear also the voice of the One who says in the heart of the human person: "You shall not steal"? More was at stake than just some general view held in society at that time: this unease in my heart came from a deeper source. Here a voice made itself heard that I regard today as a *messenger of God*. The conscience is God's messenger in our life. As a child, I heard this voice in the resonant form of a loud commandment: Do not do this! Make good what you have done wrong!

The Voice of My Conscience

Each of us ought to ask himself the question: Is this voice, which spoke so clearly to the child many years ago, still as clear today? Or do I allow this voice to be drowned out? It is possible to anesthetize the conscience; neglect can also make it like an overgrown garden. Pressures and compulsion can overlay the conscience with so much fear that it is in effect replaced by scruples and obsessions. A superficial lifestyle can reduce the conscience to a superficial level where all that counts is external appearances: if parents and society are interested only in prestige, a good facade, success, and other people's opinion, this can lead to the trivialization of a child's conscience. If it is more important to be "one of the group" than to listen to this inner voice, it can fall silent.

As recent years have shown, the devastation of people's souls in the former communist countries was a much greater tragedy than the economic devastation. "Steal, or someone will steal from you!" almost became a proverb in Eastern Europe, since the whole system of society was constructed on the principle that *everyone* was a thief. Everyone attempted to "organize things" in such a way that he kept his head above water, and theft became the ordinary way of life for an entire society. Everything was stolen, and almost everyone was compelled to steal. Besides this, the entire system was built on lies: in order to survive, people learned from an early age how to lie, and their relationship to the truth was systematically disturbed, if not actually destroyed. It was only after the collapse of communism that the consequences of all this for life in society became truly visible. There was something sad and gray about communist society, something deeply rooted in the lies that lay like a miasma over the whole of life and warped people's psychological health.

It will certainly take a long time before those countries recover, and this will not be an automatic process. It will depend on the patient work of building up those simple virtues of human life that the communist system had undermined. When we speak of the formation of the conscience, we will return to this point.

Let us now look at our Western society. Many years after my experience with the plank of wood, I began to study psychology. In keeping with the dominant school of thought at that time, there was very little place in our study of psychology for the proper understanding of conscience. The prevalent view saw the human person as a bundle of reactions and reflexes that can be measured and quantified. The human person was a machine that can be influenced, determined, and organized in whatever way one might choose. This psychology had scarcely anything to say about freedom, the soul, responsibility, or the conscience; the human person was seen as the product of his environment, his upbringing, and the influences to which he was exposed. There was an increasing tendency to regard the human person as his own legislator. He himself determines what he wants and who he is, what is good and important for him, and what he considers good or evil. In this understanding of the human person, the conscience is that which is important to *me*, that which *I* hold to be correct, that which *I* choose as the point of orientation in my life.

Conscience—Individual and More Than Individual

Understandably enough, the conflict between this view and the view of the Church has intensified in recent decades. If the conscience is that which I determine, that which seems correct to *me*, then it must be true to say that each one has his own conscience and acts in accordance with it. At this point, many of us may recall the conflict that broke out in 1968 when Pope Paul VI published the encyclical *Humanae Vitae*. For a great number of people, this took on the dimensions of a conflict of conscience. There seems to be a widening gap between the teaching of the Church and the conscience of the individual precisely in questions concerning the ethics of life. In 1968, the specific instance was the question of contraception. Many people spoke of "conscience *versus* the magisterium", and I recall any number of lively discussions where it was affirmed that the Church should not meddle in the decisions made by the conscience of believers. What entitles another person to prescribe for me how I ought to lead my life? Or what entitles the Church to formulate universal prescriptions that seem very difficult to put into practice in real life?

What is the conscience? Is it *my* conviction? Is it only what I happen to grasp at this particular moment, that of which I am certain? Or is the conscience a voice that *speaks* in me but does not *originate* in me? I believe that our task today is to reach a deeper understanding of the conscience; perhaps that would help us to see this conflict between magisterium and conscience on a profounder level. What is happening when I have pangs of conscience, when my conscience accuses me of something? Who is speaking to me then? I have pangs of conscience, but there is *another* person, *another* voice, addressing me and exhorting me: "Do not do that!" or telling me: "You ought to have done that—why did you fail to do so?" When I was a child and stole the plank, the fear I felt in my heart was the fear that I had done something wrong: for it is not right to steal. I can still remember the great relief I felt after I had brought the plank back to the workshop. There is a German proverb that rightly says: "A good conscience is a soft pillow to sleep on."

I believe that this brings us to a decisive point. The conscience is indeed something personal that only I hear; it is *my* conscience. And yet it is not merely something individual. The voice of conscience opens me up and summons me out of an existence closed in upon my own self. It gives me access to other people and to reality as a whole. It makes me aware of something I had not seen and confronts me with a reality that I did not want to perceive. My conscience says to me: "You must not steal—not even a worthless little plank!" And if I listen to this voice, I realize that this voice is present in every human heart. This is why I can tell someone else: "You must not steal!" I can appeal to *his* conscience, because I know that his conscience too is telling him: "You must not steal!"

The Task of Forming the Conscience

The conscience is a marvelously sensitive antenna, a system of finely tuned sensors that perceive reality and discern what is good, right, and true. Naturally, this presupposes that the conscience is formed and trained. A lazy conscience that has gone to seed has lost its ability to perceive things as they are, but a sensitive conscience is a wonderful instrument, helping us to be open to the summons that comes from outside ourselves. This makes it essential that we work on our conscience, training and refining it. This work lasts throughout our lives. It is correct to say that we must follow our conscience. But what kind of a conscience am I in fact following? Is it an unremarkable, primitive sort of conscience, or is it a developed conscience? Am I content with a superficial life that never goes beyond its comfortable habits?

When we sense that some event has shaken our conscience and truly awakened us, this can be the start of a deeper formation of the conscience. Let me briefly set out four steps or dimensions in this formation.

Recognize the Need for Development

First of all, I need to recognize that my conscience is underdeveloped. The saints show us how sensitive a conscience can become and how much it can perceive when it is truly developed. I must be willing to educate myself and to let myself be educated—and this means that I must be willing to let someone else challenge my conscience. If I am completely satisfied with my own life, no challenge will ever reach my conscience. But when a bad conscience or some dramatic event in my life wakes me up, this can lead to a desire to make progress and to learn more.

There is no better school than that of our Lord and Master, who told us: "Learn from me" (Mt 11:29). Jesus is the Master who teaches us how to listen to the Father's voice. No one listened to the Father better than Jesus, even in the tiniest motions of his heart. This means that for us, the school of conscience is the school of Jesus. Jesus opens our ears and our eyes. It is marvelous to study the parables of Jesus and let them echo within us. Here Jesus teaches us to look and observe; everything he says teaches us how to perceive reality. His parables are a wonderful school for the conscience: look at what nature teaches us about the mustard seed that becomes a huge tree (Mt 13:31–32) or the seed that grows on its own (Mk 4:26–29). We can learn from everything Jesus says about planting, about the vineyard, about the vinedresser (Lk 13:6–9), about the birds in the skies and the lilies of the field (Mt 6:26–30). We can also learn from his observations of people's professional work. All of this teaches us to perceive reality. Only a sensitive perception of reality can teach our conscience to be sensitive; and it is equally true that a sensitive conscience will help us to see reality more clearly.

Increase Sensitivity

The more my life is well ordered, the more sensitive my conscience will be. I must struggle to achieve good order and discipline in my life, in order that the conscience can function as it should. The simple virtues of daily living intensify our sensitivity. Consideration of others, attentiveness, overcoming one's own self, patience, discretion, humility—all this develops the conscience, making it alert and perceptive.

Seek Teachers

If I want my conscience to be sensitive—not undeveloped and primitive—then I must seek teachers, exemplary persons whose lives, words, and experience can show me the path I should take. These are "masters of life" like the saints, and often simple people are the best teachers when we seek to form a sensitive conscience. The teaching of the Church plays a role here too. We will find the solution to the conflict between the conscience and the magisterium if we are willing to trust the Church's teaching. This does not mean that I will grasp everything immediately or that every aspect will be equally clear; but I need at least this prior readiness to trust the magisterium, this conviction that I still have something to learn. Perhaps one or another doctrine of the Church contains a wisdom that I myself have not yet understood; at the very least, I will not discount the possibility that I may one day see the point of it. The pope is not the lord over my conscience, for only God—no human being—is the lord of my conscience. But the pope is a herald and a messenger of the conscience. Sometimes one has the impression that it is those outside the Church, those distant from the community of the faith, who are better able to see that the pope is truly a herald of the conscience in the whole world. The Lord has given him a special commission and has promised him the special assistance of the Holy Spirit, so that he may address our conscience and remind it of the claims God makes on us.

If I am unwilling to let myself be challenged by the word of God, then I will certainly also find it difficult to let myself be challenged by the teaching of the Church. This, however, entails the risk of identifying my conscience with my own wishes and ideas. Many psychologists hold the conscience to be an illusion; but *this* would be the real illusion, namely, that the conscience is nothing other than the ideas and wishes that are widespread in society.

Remain Attentive to Events

God speaks to us and to our conscience through events in our life, in our society, in our world. The terrorist attacks of September 11, 2001, were undeniably an event that ought to wake up our conscience. What does God want to say to us here? What does he say to me through an illness or a trial? What does he say to me through guilt? Recently, I met Karin Lamplmair, the author of the book *Ich nannte sie Nadine* (*I Named Her Nadine*). She is a young mother with two children; she let her third child be taken from her by an abortion. After this operation, she fell into a profound depression and attempted to take her life. In the course of a long and difficult process—which was, however, also filled with divine grace—she came to faith. Saint Thérèse of Lisieux played

an important role in this process. Karin found a path out of
the despair caused by the fact that she had let her third child
be taken from her and killed. She gave this child the name
Nadine and began to appeal to doctors' consciences by the
simple means of telling her own story; many reacted posi-
tively. She kept a journal of her experiences, and her book
contains many valuable testimonies.

What Karin experienced was the formation of the conscience. God led her to repentance through a dramatic event
in her life, a deep guilt that almost brought her to despair and
suicide. A decisive element in the formation of the conscience
is the experience of grace; for it is only the encounter with
the mercy of God that allows us to bear what our conscience
shows us. We cannot bear the accusations of our conscience;
but perhaps many people shut their ears to the voice of their
conscience precisely because they know nothing of grace.
They are unaware of how much God loves them. Only this
knowledge allows my conscience truly to tell me everything.
I can let it speak freely and openly, because I know that there
is not only this conscience that pronounces its verdict on me:
there is also One who looks at me and does not condemn me.
You, O Lord, are my judge—not my conscience that accuses
me. Even when our hearts condemn us, "God is greater than
our hearts" (1 Jn 3:20).

Follow Your Conscience!

I return to my starting point. The terrorists in New York
believed that they had to act as they did. They were following
their conscience. Must one always follow one's conscience? I
believe that we can now say: *Yes, one must always follow one's
conscience.* But I must always bear in mind that my conscience

can err. My conscience can never be sufficiently enlightened and sensitive. Second, I must know whether I have really acted *according to the best of my knowledge and in keeping with my conscience*. I must educate myself and seek information, and I must allow other people to correct me. Third, a true conscience can *never* tell me anything that *offends against the basic rules of human morality*. If my conscience demands that I kill innocent persons, it cannot be right. In conflicts of conscience, we must note the following three points:

1. I must ask: Am I acting according to the Golden Rule, "What you wish others to do to you, do to them too"?
2. I must always bear in mind that the end does not justify the means. It is never permissible to do evil in order that good may come.
3. Reasons of conscience may induce me to lay down my own life; but I am never permitted for reasons of conscience to take the lives of innocent persons. (I do not intend to speak here of the question of the use of violence in wars, for that would require a chapter on its own.)

The Christian hero of conscience is not the terrorist but the martyr. After long struggles, Thomas More, the great lord chancellor of England, reached the decision in conscience not to take the oath of supremacy required by Henry VIII, even though he foresaw that this decision would lead to his death. Franz Jägerstätter too followed his conscience. These men are our models. They followed the conscience that they had schooled and formed in long and intense struggles, often in the darkness of faith. And this conscience showed them the right path to take.

4

ACTING IN A HUMAN MANNER

Acting Responsibly

Come, Holy Spirit, Spirit of truth and of love, enlighten our understanding, strengthen our will, dwell in our memory, and lead us into the fullness of truth. Lead us to Christ our Lord. Amen.

The question that we shall discuss in this catechesis is elementary yet at the same time difficult: What is it that makes a human action good or bad? Since human actions cover an infinite variety of possibilities, situations, and circumstances, it is not easy to define precisely what constitutes ethical conduct. Many people before us have attempted to reflect on this question and to achieve some measure of clarity, and I should like to follow in their footsteps and to indicate—even if only in a stammering fashion—what the great masters have said about this important issue.

Father of One's Acts

The *Catechism* begins its discussion with these words:

> Freedom makes man a moral subject. When he acts deliberately, man is, so to speak, the *father of his acts*. Human

acts, that is, acts that are freely chosen in consequence of a judgment of conscience, can be morally evaluated. They are either good or evil.[1]

We have already spoken about this freedom in chapter 2. Without freedom, there is no responsibility. The stones in this cathedral[2] are not responsible for holding the building up; that is the responsibility of the master builders who joined these stones together to form a cathedral, since they are free subjects, and hence also responsible. This is why only a human being can be called the "father of his acts", a phrase that means that it is he himself who is their author. Just as parents beget children, so our actions are our "children". And we are responsible for the actions that we "bring into the world".

Not every human action is per se an ethically significant action. If I scratch my beard because something itches, this is not an action that is either good or bad but simply a reflex. There are many reflexes for which we are not called to account; but we are certainly called to account for what we do freely and in consequence of the "Judgment of conscience", as the *Catechism* says. In the preceding catechesis, we spoke of the conscience, this inner compass that tells us: "Do this!" or "Do not do that!" and that either criticizes us when something is wrong or expresses its assent when an action is good.[3] Genuinely human actions are those that proceed from our freedom, those actions of which we give an account before the tribunal of our conscience. And these can be either good or bad.

But what is good or bad? Is it so easy to give a definition? Since there is an infinite spectrum of possibilities here, it is

---

[1] *CCC* 1749.
[2] Saint Stephen's Cathedral in Vienna.—ED.
[3] Cf. *CCC* 1776–1778.

helpful to make some comments about the way we employ
the word "bad". Many events are undeniably bad but not
in a *moral* sense. Cancer is bad; a natural disaster is bad. But
these are not ethically bad. There are innumerable evils in
the world, and the most inexorable of all is death itself. What
then is the difference between such things and that which we
call "morally evil"? The *Catechism* tells us that evils exist in
the world because God has allowed them to exist; we do not
live in a perfect world but in one that is characterized by the
processes of coming into existence and passing away. There
have been tremendous developments in the cosmos, beginning with the Big Bang and including the coming into existence and the passing away of stars and galaxies, as well as the
coming into being and passing away of life on this earth. God
created our world as a world that is en route. This is why we
see comings and goings, processes of growth and decay, and
natural death in the world of living plants and animals. Look
at the marble fossils of snails that are millions of years old.
These stones that came into being from the sand of the sea
bear witness to the deaths of living creatures, and the doctrine
of our faith calls this the *physical evil* that exists in nature. It
confronts us with difficult questions: Why is there so much
cruelty in nature? Why all this coming and going? As long
as the creation has not reached perfection, this coming and
going, and this physical evil, will continue to exist.[4]

Moral evil is something completely different. This has
its source in human freedom and, as the *Catechism* says, is
"incommensurably more harmful than physical evil".[5] An illness is something bad, but sin is incomparably worse. This
is why Jesus first forgave sins and only then healed people's

---

[4] Cf. *CCC* 310, St. Thomas Aquinas, *Summa theologiae* I, 25, 6.
[5] *CCC* 311.

sicknesses. Moral evil enters the world through the door of freedom, through the freedom of an angel who turns his back on God and through the freedom of a human being who says no to God.

God allows human beings the freedom to act well or badly, and this is a great mystery. Let us reflect a little on the question of good and evil in human conduct. The *Catechism* mentions three factors that we must look at more closely, since it is these that constitute the ethical quality of our behavior. First, there is the *matter* of our actions (i.e., what we actually do); second, there is the *intention* of our actions (i.e., what we want to do, the goal we are pursuing when we do something); and third, there are the *circumstances* in which we do something.[6] Let us look at these in more detail.

The Human Action Itself

When we look at human actions, the first thing we see is not a person's intention, which often lies hidden in the heart. All we see are external actions. Sometimes we know their circumstances, but usually only to some extent; these can make a situation harder or easier. To begin with, we perceive the action itself. Let us begin with the *matter* of our action. Here both language itself and common sense are a great help.

Robbery

Let us take an example. An old lady is walking across the market square when a young man suddenly appears, snatches her handbag, and runs away. We do not use some jocular

---

[6] *CCC* 1750.

euphemism to describe what this young man does, for this is more serious than if he were to "help himself" to something from one of the market stalls: we say that he has committed a robbery.

When we call this action "robbery", we identify it as the very specific crime of violently depriving another person of his property. No one in his right mind would deny that this is per se a reprehensible action, unethical, intrinsically evil. Particular circumstances may of course make this action even worse—for example, if the old lady is handicapped, or if she suffers physical injuries when her bag is stolen. If she is killed in the course of the theft, then a whole new dimension is added, and we focus on the murder rather than on the robbery. We now speak of the criminal not simply as a robber, but as a murderer. Naturally, the question of his intention is important here, but we can be sure that he did not have a good intention! And even if we were to suppose that the young man's intention was good, that could never justify such a deed. In these circumstances, a court will look, not at his intention, but at his action, and the judge will declare him a robber or (in the worst possible case) a murderer. Objectively speaking, his action is wholly unacceptable.

Euthanasia

Let me take a second example. There is a risk in contemporary ethical discussion that we may employ harmless-sounding words to cast a veil over certain realities. Thus, we speak of *euthanasia*. This Greek word means "good death", a kind and gentle death for a person who is suffering. An old school friend of mine who is now a senior consultant in a hospital told me that he was once visited by the grandchildren of a

woman who was seriously ill with cancer and was in terrible
pain. They asked him if he could not "give her an injec-
tion to shorten her suffering". He replied: "Go and kill your
grandmother yourselves!" All at once, these sober words tore
off the linguistic veils the family had employed. For what was
actually involved? Killing someone! So let us call a spade a
spade. What is involved is the intentional taking of a human
life. As a doctor, he said: "How can you expect me to kill
your grandmother?"

Naturally, here too we can ask whether certain circumstances might justify the view of the old lady's grandchildren.
Might they not have the sincere intention of helping her in
her pain? Nevertheless, we must affirm very clearly that even
the best of intentions cannot make this a good action. This is
why it is important that we call things by their proper name,
whether good or bad. A lie is a lie. Even if I tell an untruth
out of fear, I have still lied. Adultery is adultery, even if it
is committed in the heat of passion or because one despairs
about one's own marriage.

The *Catechism* says something important about this question, although its words are perhaps not so easy to grasp.
We are to call a matter unambiguously good or bad "inso-
far as reason recognizes and judges it". Reason follows the
"objective norms of morality", because these "express the
rational order of good and evil".[7] But what are we to say
about this "rational order of morality"? Is it really true that
reason enables us to discern what is good and what is evil?
The Catholic tradition adds here that the good is that which
is in accordance with nature, while the evil is that which
contradicts nature. But what *is* human nature? And are we so
certain about what reason tells us? Is not our understanding

[7] CCC 1751.

influenced by many ideas in our culture and our society with which our own socialization has made us familiar but which might not be accepted at all in other cultures? Do not such ideas change in the course of time, so that what once was thought immodest is completely harmless today? What once was rejected out of hand is often accepted without any protest today.

Abortion

Another example shows how difficult it is to say what is truly in accordance with reason. A court of appeal in France recently published its verdict on a case where a doctor had not recognized that a child in its mother's womb was handicapped. He did not perform an abortion, nor did he advise the parents to have the child aborted. The child was born handicapped, and the parents sued the doctor for damages. The high court agreed with the parents.

Clearly, these judges were convinced that the parents' view was reasonable: Why should a handicapped child be born, if one can prevent this? This appears to be a perfectly reasonable argument to many people today, even to high court judges in a civilized country such as France, and it seems that we are obliged to ask: Are we crazy if we disagree? Are the organizations of handicapped persons who protested against this high court verdict simply out of tune with the march of progress? Or is it possible that it is these organizations that are the spokesmen of the human point of view, while the high court judges represent a profoundly inhuman point of view?

Let me mention yet another example. Prenatal diagnosis can identify with a great measure of precision the presence of Down syndrome in an unborn child. We all know how the police use computers in their hunt for criminals. What is beginning here in our own society is the use of computers in the prenatal hunt for the handicapped, and the consequence is that it will be considered antisocial, irresponsible—and hence an offense against reason—to bring a handicapped child into the world. This inevitably prompts the question: Is it not more reasonable, more humane, more natural, indeed more merciful, to spare a handicapped unborn child all the difficulties it will face in the course of its life? Such feelings are enormously widespread today, and parents who find themselves in this situation often face terrible conflicts of conscience. Gradually, a social climate is emerging in which the parents of a handicapped child risk being regarded as antisocial. The use of words such as "merciful" that veil the realities involved, the emotional confusion, and the determined effort to paint dreadful deeds in the best possible light—all these factors induce a great lack of clarity. This is why it is so necessary and urgent to look very soberly at these realities and to call things by their proper names. We must not use counterfeit language!

Nothing gives more help than faith in our search for rational clarity and sobriety. Faith does not make us unreasonable: one who follows Christ and lives in the light shed by faith gains a clear-sightedness even in the simplest matters of everyday life and will not succumb to the lies that attempt to trick him (nor to the lies he might be tempted to tell himself). He will see through all these falsehoods and recognize reality in its true colors. This, however, requires us to lead a life based on faith, so that we can free ourselves by means of such a life from self-deception, from the passions that blind us, and from the lies that make us take false paths.

We have seen the dangerous conclusions that can be drawn from prenatal diagnosis. Let me briefly put forward four simple arguments against such positions:

1. It is possible for prenatal diagnosis to be mistaken. A few days ago, I met a mother whose doctor had told her that her unborn child had Down syndrome. Nevertheless, she gave birth to the child—who was perfectly healthy. Doctors can get their diagnosis wrong!

2. Although a handicapped child is doubtless a heavy burden on a family, the child can also be a great blessing. The sixth and last child of friends of mine has Down syndrome, and the whole family agree that this child brings sunshine into their lives. Recently, I met a family who discovered the path of faith thanks to their handicapped child, because this child called into question the materialism and the obsession with success that had previously dominated their lives. Through this handicapped child, God led the family to faith.

3. We may legitimately ask, what kind of mercy is involved when a handicapped child is killed?

4. What entitles us to declare a priori what will make this child happy or unhappy? What entitles us as doctors or parents to decide whether the child should be spared the "misery" of a handicapped life? Jean Vanier, the founder of the L'Arche movement and one of the great witnesses to the Gospel in our days, discovered many decades ago how rich a life shared with handicapped persons can be and how much we can receive from them.

No doubt it remains true that a handicapped child is a burden; but does a "burden" justify killing? The primary question here is not "Will we be able to cope?" That is an understandable question, and it is perfectly acceptable, humanly speaking, when parents are faced with this new situation. But what is involved is not that kind of question but a concrete action: May we accept the killing of this child (who is perhaps handicapped)? Such an action is intrinsically wrong.

Let me clear up any potential misunderstanding by saying at this point: if an abortion is carried out, God's mercy will never exclude anyone who recognizes that he has incurred guilt. God's mercy never comes to an end, even if we make terrible mistakes. But God's mercy does not spare us from the recognition that it was a mistake—a sin.

The Intention

The second element in ethical behavior is the *intention*. Not only the external action that someone performs but also the internal intention behind this action must be evaluated. We could call this the specifically personal aspect of human actions. All that we do as human beings has an intention, a goal, a purpose. For example, let us suppose that I plan to drive out into the countryside this evening. This action has a specific purpose: I want to spend a quiet day in recollection, and I take a number of individual concrete steps to realize this intention. It is always our will that drives our behavior forward to some goal. If this will is good, then what we do is also good; but if our will is bad, then what we do is also bad. We do nothing without such an intention, purpose, or goal. Sometimes indeed, there is no immediate purpose to what we are doing; we are just pottering around, so to speak. But normally we always act for the sake of a goal, whether we are in the kitchen, at our desk in the office, or even on vacation.

Multiple Motives

Why did I become a priest? I became a priest in order to follow Christ and to serve other people, and I believe that everyone who has chosen this path could say the same. But

is that really the case? Was I really acting from such noble
motives? Was I not pursuing other goals too? Is it not the
case that in almost all our actions, a whole bundle of intentions and motivations comes into play? Even in the stories
of the vocation of the apostles, there are subsidiary motives.
Perhaps one reason why they left everything and followed
Jesus was a yearning for adventure; or perhaps it was simple
curiosity: "Rabbi, where are you staying?" "Come and see"
(Jn 1:38ff.). Perhaps another factor was the desire for a good
career: for if this Jesus really is the Messiah, we may get good
jobs at his court. All this may indeed have played a role; but
when all the apostles, one after the other, laid down their
lives as martyrs for Christ, their intention had been purified
in the fire of tribulation to such an extent that they could
truly make their own the words Peter spoke to Jesus after
Easter: "Lord, you know everything; you know that I love
you" (Jn 21:17).

Many motives contribute to what we do, but pure motivations also exist. When a fireman rushes out in an emergency,
we are entitled to assume that he does this simply because he
wants to help. No vanity is involved, no subsidiary motives
come into play here, even if it may be the case that he joined
the fire department solely because it was customary in his vil-
lage for all the men to join. It is wonderful when we encounter a pure deed in which the external action and the internal
intention correspond completely. When someone performs
a good action out of a pure heart and intention, this is truly
beautiful.

Let me return to my first example. Let us suppose that
another young man has seen the first young man attacking the
old lady. He rushes up and protects her from the would-be
thief. He has acted speedily and intervened without delay,
and he has protected the old lady. We find such an action

truly praiseworthy: he has acted courageously and decisively, perhaps at considerable risk to himself. He has risked his own life in order to protect this woman. We are right to praise such "everyday heroes".

But what brings someone to do the right deed at the right moment? There is more here than just this momentary action. This individual action, which is so correct and convincing, probably has to be seen in a larger context. There is a prehistory to this spontaneous assistance where one person puts his own life at risk, just as there is a prehistory to the other person who averts his gaze—"That is none of my business!"—and then turns his back and scuttles off. Both reactions to the situation are connected with the development, or lack of development, of an ethical character.

Ethical Personality

The intention of our actions is determined to a very high degree by the quality of our ethical personality as a whole. The more clearly this personality is developed, the more straightforward and correct my individual actions will be, the more upright my intention will be, and the more harmony there will be in the basic orientation of the various spheres of my life. If this total orientation of my life is as it should be and gradually takes on clearer outlines, my individual actions will acquire a greater luminosity and beauty, since the individual act will be the expression of my total existential attitude. When my life is oriented with ever-greater clarity to its final goal, in other words, to God—"Thy will be done!"—then it takes on an inner luminosity. This basic orientation is like a magnet that imposes order on the individual iron filings and draws them in the same direction. My life then takes on coherence, stability, and ethical beauty, and this can be seen even in the small details of my everyday living. This does not mean that everything is always directly and totally oriented to God. When I stir the pot in the kitchen or type on my computer keyboard, these actions do not always immediately envisage God. But everything I do takes on an inner luminosity and purity—the quality that we admire in upright persons.

When I speak of "upright persons", I am always reminded of the old janitor in our monastery in Fribourg. For me, he was the embodiment of an upright person. He was physically upright too, and he had a marvelously upright attitude until the day he died. There was nothing devious about him. Everything he did was right, somehow, whether he was working at his carpenter's bench, sweeping the driveways around the house, sitting in the porter's lodge, drinking a glass of cognac, or lighting one of his little cigars. He was an upright man.

This inner orientation can disintegrate for various reasons. Our life is a continuous struggle to achieve this inner orientation and to practice it in what we do. An action that is externally correct can become a bad action if our intention is wrong. In the Sermon on the Mount, Jesus gives the examples of praying, fasting, and almsgiving. All this is undeniably good, but if we do these things in order to be seen by other people, out of vanity and the desire for recognition, then what we do is worthless. Indeed, Jesus says clearly that our actions become bad (Mt 6:2–18): an objectively good action can be corrupted by a bad intention and thus become a bad action. If I do something objectively bad with a good intention, it does not thereby become a good action. I may steal in order to help the poor, but theft remains theft: it does not become a good deed. I may lie in order to extricate someone from a tricky situation, but falsehood remains falsehood. The end does not justify the means.

The Circumstances

This brings us to the final point, the *circumstances*. Everything we do takes place in the context of an infinite number of circumstances. Traditionally, these are identified by means of these questions: Who? With what? What? Where? Why? How? When? In a specific case, the circumstances can turn an action that is good per se into a bad action. For example, it is good to pray the rosary. But if I arrive at the scene of a traffic accident and wander around praying the rosary instead of helping the injured, I am doing something despicable. (This point is made by the philosopher Robert Spaemann in his introduction to Thomas Aquinas' treatise on ethical conduct.) No doubt, there is a difference between a small and a large theft. The small theft is not as serious as the large-scale robbery; yet each is theft. If I tell a lie because I am afraid I may be killed, my words remain a lie, but my guilt is very slight. We speak here of "extenuating circumstances". The totality of circumstances can make a situation more or less serious; but the action itself remains what it is.

What is the consequence for our lives? Our faith tells us: "Seek first the kingdom of God, and everything else shall be yours as well" (cf. Mt 6:33). We are expected to choose the basic orientation, and one who attempts to orient his life to the will of God will discern more and more clearly in the details of his individual actions the form taken by the good. This requires us to structure our intentions aright and to master our passions, in order that our heart may be in the right place. If our basic orientation is correct, our individual actions will likewise be correct (see chapter 5). We are helped in this effort by the virtues, in other words, those attitudes that make it possible for us to make the right decisions in individual situations (see chapter 6). It is obvious that the young man who rushed to the help of the old lady had developed the virtue of courage in his life, and this enabled him to act correctly at the decisive moment. Without virtues, correct behavior is impossible. They are, so to speak, the buttresses that keep our lives upright.

5

WITHOUT PASSIONS, ETHICAL LIVING IS IMPOSSIBLE

Lord, almighty Father, through the baptism of your Son you have shown us the path that makes us children of God. Lead us along this path all the days of our life until we reach your glory. We make our prayer through Christ our Lord. Amen.

At first sight, the subject of this catechesis is rather unusual: the question of the passions and ethical living. What do we mean by "passions"? And how are they connected to morality?

Defining the Passions

When a topic seems unusual, it is always a good idea to begin by looking at a dictionary. The striking thing is that the word "passion" has a rather negative ring today. The standard German dictionary gives the following definition: "The passions are emotions that find expression in conduct that reason finds it difficult to control. These emotional states aim at something, desire something, or pursue some goal." Some examples from everyday language are then given:

"a blind passion"

"passion holds sway over someone, sweeps him away, takes hold of him"

"stirring up the passions of the crowd"—something that happens in the political sphere

"unleashing the passions"

"he is a plaything of his passions"

"a person free of passions (a sober and prudent person)"

We also find more positive instances: "He has worked passionately (with great commitment) for the realization of this project."

We also read of "a passion for something that one continually tries to get hold of and possess; a passion for a particular activity, to which one devotes oneself wholeheartedly": for example, "riding is his passion" or "his passion is automobiles."

We also read of "discovering a passion for something; cultivating a passion for something; succumbing to a passion for gambling; he is a passionate collector; he practices his hobby with genuine passion; she was passionately fond of the theater."

The dictionary speaks further of "an attraction to another person that is expressed in intense emotions, in a vehement and unbridled yearning to possess the other; a wild, great, stormy passion; to be seized by an intense passion for someone."

The adjective "passionate" is qualified as "very emotional, placing great emphasis on the feelings, not governed by reason ... he is filled with a passionate hatred."

A little later, under the word "dispassionate", we read: "free from emotional influences, sober, governed by reason: he is a completely dispassionate man."

We also read, however: "he seems far too dispassionate (too cold, without empathy)"; "free of passion: the existential ideal of this man is to become completely dispassionate."

The Passions and Reason

It is obvious that the "passions" are generally understood here as something irrational and that "passionate" is seen as the antithesis of "governed by reason". If this is the case, then there cannot be any ethical passions. Morality is concerned with reason and responsibility, and if passion is irrational, emotions have no place in morality. We have, however, also noted the dictionary explanation of "dispassionate" as "too cold, without empathy". Is such a freedom from passion truly a goal to be aimed at? Is it desirable to be a person who is cold and without empathy? Is not the capacity for empathy one element in a rounded and mature personality? Do we not consider one who lacks empathy to be a heartless person, inhuman, perhaps indeed pathologically ill?

I attended a lecture in a psychiatric clinic one day in 1967. The professor presented the case of a patient whose wife, in a fit of mental illness, had hacked off both hands of her child. This terrible event was much talked about in the media at the time. It was evaluated from the outset as a pathological and sick action, not as the fruit of a rational decision, and so the woman was committed to the psychiatric clinic. A few days later, the husband too was brought to the clinic, because it had been observed that he showed no emotional reaction to this dreadful event. The doctors and the court judged this attitude to be potentially pathological, and so they committed him to the clinic.

If we seek to develop a mature personality, a lack of passion is a hindrance. A rounded personality needs the right amount of heart, feelings, emotions, and—as we shall see—passions. Naturally, a rounded and mature personality needs reason and the will—but also a passion for the good. Can we imagine a passionless saint? Can we imagine a Teresa of Avila, with all the energy she employed in her monastic reform and with her love of Christ, as a dispassionate woman, or a Francis of Assisi without the passion for poverty and for the imitation of Christ that led him to take the existentially decisive step of embracing a leper? How then were the saints passionate? They were certainly not the hapless victims of their passions; but they were just as certainly not dispassionate. How are we to understand the "passions"?

When we hear this word, we often think spontaneously of something we must struggle against, and this is certainly correct: we must learn to tame and control the passions. With some passions, we come to point where we must put them "to death" in order to be truly free of them, as Saint Paul says (Col 3:5). But are there not passions that lend us wings—for example, enthusiasm? Enthusiasm is not merely the product of a recognition on the part of reason that something or other is important, or of a decision on the part of the will to strive to put into practice what reason has discerned. Feelings are involved too!

One example is the choice of my way of life. If someone decides to become a nurse, is this exclusively a matter for reason? Doubtless, rational arguments will play their part, but it is unlikely that this profession will be chosen without a passionate desire to help people who are in need. At the very least, one will feel attracted to this profession. Perhaps the person thinks quite simply: "I enjoy doing this." And that is a genuine argument: if I enjoy doing something, this may legitimately tilt the balance in favor of the decision to spend my life doing so, or at least to take a deeper interest in this kind of work.

Is it permissible to say: "I enjoy this profession"? We will see that without a certain amount of enjoyment, human existence cannot be fully rounded and harmonious. The contrary example is eloquent: if someone says that he takes no pleasure in his professional work, he will scarcely have any joy in it, and he will probably not be very good at what he does. There is something missing in the humanity of one who does good without feeling any pleasure thereby. Is there then such a thing as ethical pleasure? The Church's tradition, above all as represented by Saint Thomas Aquinas, the great master, unhesitatingly says yes. Joy and pleasure in the good do exist, and this pleasure in doing what is good is the strongest magnet attracting us to do good. One can even ask: Is there such a thing as a good and moral action that is devoid of pleasure and passion? This brings us to the subject of the present catechesis. In the *Catechism*, we read in the chapter titled "The Morality of the Passions": "The human person is ordered to beatitude by his deliberate acts: the passions or feelings he experiences can dispose him to it and contribute to it."[1] Passions or feelings can help us find our path to the goal of our life, namely, eternal bliss.

The Passions in Our Life

Let us begin with a remark of a more historical character. There is little place for the passions either in Catholic moral philosophy or in modern philosophy, and where they are

---

[1] *CCC* 1762.

mentioned, they are usually seen in a negative light. They are considered as hindrances that disturb reason in its attempt to do what is right and good; and one must fight against them. In classical times, the Stoic philosophers maintained that the passions were an illness of the soul. Illnesses must be healed, and this means that we must free ourselves of the passions. Some religious traditions have their starting point in this view of the human person; very many Buddhists, for example, hold that the human person should aim as far as possible to lay aside all the passions. The underlying anthropology is not that of Judaism and Christianity.

Saint Thomas Aquinas wrote an extensive treatise on the human passions, a text with a tremendous vitality that offers a wealth of insight into all the interconnections and articulations of the human emotions. One could well recommend it to modern psychologists; I believe that they could learn a great deal from what Thomas says.

The emotions are an important component of our life. What is the connection between emotions, feelings, and passions (on the one hand) and morality, with a successful human life (on the other)? Saint Thomas devotes so much space to this question because he is convinced that the human person is a living unity of body and soul and that everything in the human person is significant: not only the intellect, the will, or the spirit, but also the feelings, the powers of the senses, and the body itself. Saint Paul says that everything must be a unity—body, soul, and spirit—that gives glory to God (1 Cor 12:12–31a; Eph 4:4; 1 Thess 5:23). Everything is important for a human life: we are not a "ghost in a machine", nor are we an "intellect in an animal". Our emotions are not animal but human, even if they do resemble the emotions of animals in certain respects. We are human beings; our emotions and feelings are human, and indeed ought to be human. They are good and well ordered to the extent that they *are* human. We are not called to holiness only with our understanding and our will but also with our feelings, emotions, and passions. The entire world of our feelings is to set out upon the path of sanctification. This world of our feelings influences us; at the same time, we are called to shape it and order it.

When we read the Gospels, we do not encounter our Master and Lord, Jesus Christ, as a dispassionate figure. Let me mention only a few passages that show us the entire spectrum of feelings in the life of Jesus. We are told several times that he weeps and has strong emotions. We hear of the tears that are produced by his grief: Jesus weeps over his friend Lazarus (Jn 11:35); he weeps in pain and grief over Jerusalem (Lk 19:41). Jesus can exult in joy, for example, because the Father has hidden his mysteries from the wise and learned and revealed them to the little ones and infants (Lk 10:21). We often hear about Jesus' compassion; the Hebrew word in the background of these passages means literally "entrails", indicating that Jesus is moved by compassion in the innermost depths of his heart, for example, when he sees the crowds who have followed him to the shore of the lake while he was traveling in the disciples' boat: "As he landed he saw a great throng, and he had compassion on them, because they were like sheep without a shepherd" (Mk 6:34).

When Jesus sees the widow outside the gates of the city of Nain, as her only son is being carried out for burial, he has compassion on her (Lk 7:13). There are many other texts that speak of his compassion; but he also feels anger when he sees the traders in the Temple and makes a whip of cords, overturns their tables, and drives them out (Jn 2:14–16; Mt 21:12–13; Mk 11:15–17; Lk 19:45–46). When he wishes to heal a man with a withered hand on a sabbath day in the synagogue, he looks around and observes how hard are the hearts of those present. The evangelist writes: "He looked around at them with anger" (Mk 3:5). Jesus knows what it is to be seized by a vehement emotion: "Now is my soul troubled", he says before the Last Supper (Jn 12:27). He also knows fear, the terribly profound fear of death that leads him to sweat blood in the garden of Gethsemane, this extraordinary physical manifestation of his inner state (Lk 22:44).

He experiences yearning: "I have earnestly desired to eat this Passover with you", he says in the upper room (Lk 22:15). The yearning in the heart of Jesus is a powerful expression of his emotion, of his passionate longing. A paradoxical, surprising revelation of this is his yearning for the coming of the kingdom of God, for what he calls "the hour". In concrete terms, this means that Jesus yearns to lay down his life. How can he long for suffering, yearn for something that is so deeply repulsive to the human person—so repulsive that he sweats blood in his agony, in his fear of dying, when this hour finally comes? Here is a whole wealth of feelings and emotions, and we must try to detach the word "passion" from its modern negative connotations and simply take it for what it originally means: the passions are the expression of the world of our emotions.

It is not only in the Lord that we find the entire palette of human emotions. We encounter them in his disciples too, most of all in the letters of the apostle Paul, who says a great deal about his emotions. For example, he writes "with many tears" (2 Cor 2:4); he writes in anger at the bad conduct of the Christian communities (Gal 4:8–20); he compares his concern for the believers to the concern a mother shows her children (1 Thess 2:7); he expresses his joy (2 Cor 2:3; 7:4; Phil 1:4; 4:1; Col 2:5; 1 Thess 2:19ff.; 3:9) but also his annoyance and his disappointment at the conduct of other apostles (Gal 2:11–14).

The Vital Force of the Senses

What are we to make of all these emotions? What does our faith say about them? What does the Christian experience of life tells us? One thing is certain: unlike Stoicism, and perhaps also Buddhism, Christianity does not require us to get rid of the emotions or deny them: for otherwise, Jesus would not have displayed them. It is clear that we must primarily allow ourselves to be guided by the will and reason, for that is what constitutes us as human beings. But these are not the only components of the human person. We also have the vital force of the senses, which are not located in the understanding.

If one observes a child in the first year of his life, before he can speak, one will see first of all the vital force of the senses in an elementary form: pleasure and displeasure, reaching out to take one thing and shrinking back from another. With his senses, the child finds his way into the world, getting to know it by tasting, sucking, and touching, as well as by seeing and hearing. The child reacts with pleasure to what he finds pleasurable, and with displeasure to what he finds unpleasant—often with screams. These initial experiences establish the basic pattern for our entire life, which accompanies us into old age. Even when reason is fully awake and the will has taken over the reins of government, these fundamental tendencies to pleasure and displeasure remain.

When Saint Thomas speaks of the emotions involved in these two tendencies, he gives them the names "love" and "hate". We strive toward that which is pleasant, and this prompts the feeling of love and devotion in us; we ward off that which is unpleasant, and we may call this hate. In a little child, all this takes place instinctively, but as one grows older, one may no longer simply react instinctively, and a great deal of education consists precisely in assisting this process. A schoolchild can no longer simply be swayed by pleasure or displeasure: he must sit down at his desk and work at his lessons. We must discipline our emotions and reactions and subordinate them to the will and reason. I cannot simply act and react in accordance with pleasure or displeasure; my duty at the moment, or a longer-term goal I want to attain, requires me to overcome boredom and disinclination.

Does this mean that pleasure and displeasure no longer have any importance in my life? No, for joy can make pleasure greater, deeper, and stronger; and the disgust provoked by something evil can lend much more depth and strength to a spontaneous displeasure. Initially, it may be only a spontaneous aversion, but intellectual and spiritual insight into the reality of evil can transform this into a profound emotional horror. Much of our ethical living is located within this interplay between our feelings, our reason, and our will. Sometimes we experience this as a conflict full of tension, but often there is a mutual enrichment.

There are deep intellectual joys that also find expression in sensuous delight, in a joy that (as Saint Thomas says) overflows like a fountain and takes hold of our senses. But the opposite experience also exists: in the midst of great external discomfort of the senses, the body, or the mind, in great anguish of soul, in physical pain, or in psychological distress, one can nevertheless taste spiritual joy. This is one of the most mysterious aspects of the spiritual life: precisely while our soul is bowed down, we can experience a joy that does not have any effect on the psychological and emotional dimensions of our person yet is a perfectly genuine spiritual joy. In a celebrated text, Saint Thérèse of Lisieux speaks precisely of this experience: she reflects on how our Lord suffered the most terrible pains in Gethsemane and on the cross, not only in his body but also in his mind—and yet he remained bound to his Father in the deepest joy.

Desire and Aggression

Let us now take one further step. Saint Thomas attempts, in the light of the great tradition to which he refers, to order the world of the feelings, and he makes a distinction between two great categories of passion, both of which can be found in all living beings—plants, animals, and human beings. All living beings seek what does them good and resist what harms them. Thomas uses the term *concupiscibilis*, "the power of desire", to designate the yearning for what is in harmony with oneself, accords with one's nature, and does one good. Every animal does this; the same is true of plants and human beings.

There is a second category of feelings: we must face up to things that threaten us and actively resist things that are harmful. Our body does this when it mobilizes its powers of resistance, its immune system, to fight against an infection. This too is common to plants, animals, and human beings. Saint Thomas calls this *irascibilis*, "the power of resistance". Today, we might use the word "aggression", although it is not meant here in a negative sense.

The *power of desire* manifests itself in spontaneous attractions or aversions, in pleasure or discomfort, love or hatred, joy or sadness; it draws us to that which is good and frightens us away from that which is harmful. This fundamental power of desire reacts automatically in us and is an important criterion helping us to recognize (or at least to sense) what is good for us and what is harmful. We possess a sensitivity to what does us good, and we need this feeling in order to find the right orientation in our life.

The second basic power, *aggression,* is more difficult. Saint Thomas gives the simple example of an animal following its desire and looking for something to eat. A predator becomes aggressive and takes risks in order to find food; it incurs danger and exposes itself to a struggle that may turn out badly for the predator itself. We are continually confronted with similar situations since ready-cooked meals do not fly into our mouths, so to speak; we must fight against dangers, opposition, difficulties, hostilities. In many ways, our life is a struggle. Saint Thomas calls the power of the soul that confronts all this the *irascibilis* (literally, "the power of anger"), which empowers us to tackle difficult tasks without being crushed in advance by the extent and difficulty of the problems involved. The *irascibilis* also includes the ability to assess how much power I need in order to master a difficulty. Ultimately, this power too is concerned with something good that one wants to achieve. If your desire is to get good marks in an examination, this goal, the successful conclusion of your studies, is itself good; but in order to achieve the good end, you must take great pains and mobilize your inner forces; you must renounce many pleasures and postpone many things you would like to do. Every athlete in training knows that he must renounce a great many things if he is to win a gold medal. The power of desire is spontaneous, but the power to tackle difficulties, the power of aggression, demands that I overcome myself and transcend myself; I must evaluate the difficulties correctly, without either overestimating or underestimating my own abilities. The power of aggression demands strategic activity that is clearly directed toward a goal. We can see this in animals too, when they encounter some difficulty: blind aggression does not help.

A Dominican confrere of mine wrote a monumental work of scholarship over the course of many years. He used to say:

"I have invested all my *irascibilis* in this work." He employed all his powers of resistance and all his passionate energy in order to realize this goal. He renounced many other things, perhaps very beautiful things—visits to other places, interesting books and conversations—in order to write this great work. For there is no great work without a strong *irascibilis*. The same is true of the athletes who need vigorous training in order to be successful. This can be achieved only by one who conquers his own self, his craving for comfort, and his disinclination for hard effort and who willingly shoulders the strenuous labors involved.

Passions and Holiness

The Christian tradition acknowledges that there is no holiness without the fuel of these two passions—powerful desire and powerful aggression. Holiness does not consist of these passions, but it is possible only where these two powers are present and come into play.

Naturally, the path of holiness and the path of morality require us to do more than overcome material and psychological difficulties (such as those that face an athlete); we must also prove our worth in spiritual struggles. We are confronted not only with external vicissitudes but also by our own inclination to evil, and an initiation into the Christian life is necessary if this struggle is to be won. The simple exercises of which I have spoken are the presupposition, the human basis if you will, without which there is no path to holiness. But the Christian path takes one further step. When Saint Thomas speaks of the interior attitudes that correspond to this power of aggression, he focuses above all on *hope*. He does not refer here to the theological virtue as such but simply to the vital human power of hope, which consists in the confidence that one will be able to tackle difficulties and overcome them. The opposite quality is a dejection that can go as far as despair, leading one to abandon the work half-done, to run away, and to lose confidence in oneself because one is afraid of difficulties. Hope includes boldness, and Saint Thomas speaks in this context of the anger that we have seen when Jesus cleanses the Temple. All of this belongs to what Thomas calls the power of the *irascibilis* and forms its natural basis.

If it is true that the human person is a unity of body and soul, it follows that the emotions belong not only to the basic equipment with which human life is furnished; they belong also to human morality. We need the emotions if our life is not to disintegrate. In the same way, the simple experiences of pleasurable fulfillment are necessary for our life: food, sleep, health, the right relationship to our sexuality. Saint Thomas says that a life without pleasure is unimaginable—and such a life would not be human.

But can one trust one's feelings? Can I entrust myself to them? I believe that we must make a distinction here. It is very important to grant admittance to one's feelings: if you love only with your head, you take the risk that it will drown out the voice of your feelings, which might have something important to tell you. The feelings can be a sensitive signpost. Often, my feelings warn me of some danger long before my intellect has perceived it. Desire, striving, yearning, longing—all this can indeed deepen in us a sensitivity toward what is right, a kind of intuition vis-à-vis the good, and this has a great deal to do with our feelings.

Nevertheless, we must make a distinction: not every feeling and every passion is a reliable compass. Feelings can also lead to confusion and error; they can be the source of vices and sins. The passions can get the better of me. No one should imagine that he is invulnerable here. We can fall victim to our passions; even worse, we can make our reason and our will the servants of our passions, although it is reason and the will that ought to be governing the passions. This is why it is important to make distinctions, to correct, to struggle, and to pursue the task of integration, in order that the emotions may more and more enrich the human personality as a whole, bringing their influence upon us to make us creative.

Our passions have their own language, their own logic. They are not simply the dictate of our reason and will: if, for example, I say that I must take account of another person's feelings, this is not only the work of reason. It is the work of the heart. And perhaps it is this biblical word "heart" that shows us most clearly what is involved here. The *heart* is meant to show us the right path, but this presupposes that my heart and my feelings are well ordered and that my passions are not chaotic. A disordered life results in disordered passions. This is why we must cultivate good habits, in our emotions as in other aspects of daily living. When we develop good habits, we develop the virtues.

Training the Emotions

How can one support, train, and cultivate one's feelings, gifts, and emotions in such a way that they bear the fruit of good habits? Christ taught his disciples how this was possible. In his person, they could see how one imposes order on the feelings and passions, and how they are to be structured aright. Jesus not only imparted a doctrine to them, but he displayed his teaching in his own exemplary life, so that they could see in him what compassion and an open heart really mean. Above all, they could see in him what it means to transform one's feelings into love for one's enemies. This is impossible on the natural level; I cannot love my foe spontaneously. But when Jesus turns our heart around through his Spirit and gives us the life that he himself led, we can begin to do something that our human feelings on their own could never achieve: we ourselves can love our enemies, and our emotions can be not only well ordered but oriented to the kingdom of God, to the happiness that Jesus wants to give us. This is possible! We see this transformation in all the saints, who imposed an order on their emotions in such a way that they wholeheartedly served the kingdom of God. To respond not with hatred but with love to the unpalatable fact that someone is my enemy—*this* is the path for our feelings and passions that Jesus wishes to teach us.

6

"VIRTUES MAKE PEOPLE GOOD"

*Come, Holy Spirit, Spirit of truth and of love, enlighten our
understanding, strengthen our will, dwell in our memory, and
lead us into the fullness of truth, that truth which is Christ our
Lord. Amen.*

If then you have been raised with Christ, seek the things that
are above, where Christ is, seated at the right hand of God.
Set your minds on things that are above, not on things that
are on earth. For you have died, and your life is hidden with
Christ in God. When Christ who is our life appears, then you
also will appear with him in glory.

Put to death therefore what is earthly in you: immoral-
ity, impurity, passion, evil desire, and covetousness, which is
idolatry. On account of these the wrath of God is coming. In
these you once walked, when you lived in them. But now
put them all away: anger, wrath, malice, slander, and foul talk
from your mouth. Do not lie to one another, seeing that you
have put off the old man with his practices and have put on
the new man, who is being renewed in knowledge after the
image of his creator.... Put on then, as God's chosen ones,
holy and beloved, compassion, kindness, lowliness, meek-
ness, and patience, forbearing one another and, if one has a
complaint against another, forgiving each other.... And over

all these put on love, which binds everything together in perfect harmony. (Col. 3:1–10, 12–14)

The New Life

In this catechesis, we will speak about the virtues; Paul lists some of these in the text we have just read. Through baptism, we have become new people (Rom 6:4); in baptism, we have clothed ourselves in Christ (Gal 3:27). What is involved here is a new life. At the same time, quite simple virtues are mentioned, such as patience, humility, kindness, and mercy. So what are we to make of these human virtues—both the natural virtues and those that are specifically Christian? How are these two categories related?

Let us begin with what we said about the passions. We have seen that they can be threatening; we have noted the power they have; but we have also spoken of their positive vigor. Like the charioteer's horses, the passions need to be bridled. If they are unchecked, they can rampage destructively, growing beyond all measure and thus becoming inhuman. Something decisively human is missing in a person who knows no restraints and is unbridled in his consumption; in his eating and drinking; in his desire for sexual pleasure; in his struggle to attain recognition, honor, power, or success. When someone lacks all inner restraint, we do not regard his life as successful in human terms. One who shrinks back in fear as soon as he encounters any obstacle, one who immediately tacks to the prevailing wind, lacks something essential to a complete and good human existence; and the same is true of one who all too easily flies into a rage and shouts and screams. We use words like "depraved" to describe people who allow their passions to control their lives. Irascibility is a vice, as are pride and the chronic thirst for recognition and praise. Those who squander their money are just as much in thrall to a vice as the misers who gloat coldly over their hoard. The vices are bad companions. They are like the ruts on a forest path that are so deep that an automobile can scarcely make its way between the trees. The vices are ruts that keep us imprisoned on the wrong path. They leave the wrong kind of imprint on our lives—unlike the good habits that we call virtues.

The word "virtue" is unfashionable today and is indeed sometimes mocked and ridiculed. But if we look back across Western history to the pre-Christian philosophers, we see that they spoke with great enthusiasm of the virtues, and we are impressed even today by the way in which the pagan philosophers Plato and Aristotle portray the life of one who knows how to practice self-control and is upright and well ordered in his own self, not merely for one moment, but consistently. It is the virtues that make a person upright in the long term. In this catechesis, we will speak of the simple human virtues, of the Christian virtues, and of how these are related.

Virtue as a Skill

The simplest definition of "virtue" that I know is given by Saint Thomas Aquinas, one of the greatest masters in the art of reflection on the virtues. He dedicated a large section of his voluminous writings to an exact analysis of these fundamental human attitudes, and he puts the matter very simply: "A virtue is *that which makes the person who possesses it good*" (in Latin, *quae bonum facit habentem*). Virtues make people good. A good person is not someone who occasionally performs a good deed or is decent and responsible now and again; a good person is one who *is* good. Is this possible for a human being? Can we be good? The old pagan masters were convinced of the possibility that thanks to the virtues, certain attitudes become natural to us. They become our very own, to such an extent that they make us genuinely good. Let us look at this in greater detail.

The pre-Christian masters show us that the virtues cover a very wide spectrum. There are ethical virtues and intellectual virtues but also practical virtues, which we might call our "craftsmen's skills". In this context, Aristotle is fond of the image of the craftsman. A carpenter who has learned his trade, first as an apprentice, then as an associate, and finally as a master, knows the work that is required of him. It is "in" him, for it has become natural to him. A baker who knows his trade has amassed his knowledge and practical skills through years of work. It is this kind of experience that makes one a master. Such persons are genuinely masters in their own professional sphere, and they find their work easy; but if you set down one who is not a baker in front of a trough of dough, the product will most likely be sweat rather than a good loaf, and one who is not a carpenter is not going to produce any masterpieces at the workbench. For one who has learned his trade, however, his work has become second nature.

This work may in fact be very demanding, but it brings joy to the one who knows how to do it aright. The craftsman is satisfied when the object of his toil is finished and is as it should be. I recall looking at a finely chiseled Gothic tombstone in a church with a stonemason, who stood there full of admiration. His admiration was much deeper than mine could be, because he could infer from his own experience how competent the medieval master must have been.

"Practice makes perfect." You can acquire a skill in some sphere or other; but if you do not practice this skill over a long period of time, it gets rusty and may in fact disappear. This is true of the foreign languages we learn: if we do not practice them, they get rusty. This is true of musical instruments that we once learned to play but then neglect for years on end. This is how skills atrophy. A great deal of practice and continuous work are necessary to achieve and to retain a special ability, whether in the sphere of practical work, technical skills, or the arts. It suffices here to think of airline pilots. And this kind of skill inclines the one who possesses it to put it into practice: one who plays the piano well is happy to sit down at the instrument, perhaps in order to impress other people but often simply to experience the pleasure of playing the piano.

When we speak of virtue as a "skill", we mean something acquired by practice, an ability that has become one's own, or indeed has become a second nature. It empowers us and inclines us to act in a particular manner, and the outcome is joy; Saint Thomas notes that when we put into practice the skills that we have acquired, we find pleasure and joy in doing so. At the same time, we know that all these abilities of which we have been speaking—in the fields of the arts, technology, or craftsmanship—may make you a good baker, a good pilot, or a good computer expert. But they do not suffice to make you a good person.

Developing the Virtues

A successful human existence requires something more than the training, developing, and structuring of individual competencies, namely, the development of the entire human person, of the personality with its ethical and human qualities. And precisely this is the aim of the virtues in the human person: they seek to make us whole persons, rounded off,

successful. How does this occur? How do we impose a structure on our life? How does one become a good person?

Is not the human person naturally good? Did not God
make him good? Can we not simply allow children to grow
up and develop without disturbance from outside?

Here we find two points of view that have often been
played off against one another in recent decades. This has had
very concrete consequences, although I must say that it seems
to me that life itself has refuted both standpoints.

The starting point of the "antiauthoritarian education" that
flourished in the 1960s and 1970s was the assumption that
the human person is naturally good. One need only allow
him to grow, and he will turn out well. Everything that clips
his wings, imposes boundaries, or checks his development in
an authoritarian manner, everything that smells of coercion,
must be avoided, so that the child can develop freely. I imagine that many parents know only too well that the results
of such an education (or noneducation) are catastrophic,
since although children certainly do not need an authoritarian education, they do need authority and formation. Adults
too need boundaries; our bad inclinations need to encounter
resistance. And we must also be *taken seriously*—the absence
of this is certainly one fundamental mistake of the antiauthoritarian education—in our struggle to find our own path
in life, which must accept the confrontation with other paths
and with other freedoms. The human person must experience boundaries that allow him to grow. Ultimately, a noneducation in the antiauthoritarian style fails to take children
seriously. It is woefully inadequate for parents and teachers
simply to abandon me to my instincts and feelings, my whims
of the moment. This cannot bear good fruit!

There was another path too, an authoritarian education
that understood education in virtue primarily as "drill". I can

still recall words my father used: "You have to drill them until they turn sixteen." I am convinced that this view too is wrong; the antiauthoritarian education was surely a reaction against an understanding of education as hammering the correct modes of conduct into children and inculcating the appropriate responses in them. We have all heard of the dog of the Russian psychologist Ivan Pavlov (d. 1936). Before the dog was fed, a bell was rung; and Pavlov noted that even when the ringing was not in fact followed by food for the dog, the animal's mouth began to water. This is known as a "Pavlovian response"—something unnatural, the product of training. Are the virtues Pavlovian responses? Are they modes of conduct that have been hammered into us, ideas about respectable behavior that have been instilled in us? That would be a caricature.

It is of course true that virtues are formed by repeatedly doing what is correct and good. If your parents tell you often enough to stand up straight, you get accustomed to standing upright, and this becomes natural for you. There are such things as good habits, and there is nothing wrong with acquiring these, even if that means an external drill. Unfortunately, vices too come into being through habitual practice, and they become bad habits unless we fight against them. Gossip or slander can develop from a habit to a vice; the vice of wrath establishes a foothold when our anger keeps on blazing up and we do nothing to quell it. Naturally, there is a very important difference between vices and virtues, which do not exist on the same level, as if it were a matter of indifference whether one trained oneself in good or bad modes of conduct. Vices are detrimental to our humanity, whereas virtues build it up. Vices do not come into being through the toil of practice but by continually letting oneself go; virtues, on the other hand, are often the fruit of a wearisome, patient work of construction. Vices grow through neglect, like weeds in an overgrown garden. Virtues grow when they are cultivated and worked at; they need constant attention.

Although this patient, continuous work at the virtues possesses a certain resemblance to drill, it is most certainly not an external process of accustoming oneself to some specific patterns of conduct. It is of course true that if when you are a child your parents tell you a hundred times to say thank you, you will get accustomed to do so; and if we have been taught to stand up and give an elderly person our seat on the bus or to greet people politely, these external forms provide the kind of external scaffolding that we need, as human beings of flesh and blood. The good habits in which we have been trained are like the skeleton of bones that supports the entire body, and they are very helpful for life in society. Things are much more pleasant when we greet one another politely than when we merely follow our passing moods. Here, however, we are still in the realm of good habits—we have not yet come to the true virtues.

Virtue in the Innermost Depths
of the Human Person

Virtues are more than good habits. They are the inner structure of the person, not something externally added on but inner forces that shape our whole lives. They are not an external corset, not even the coercion that I may sometimes need. Virtues are inner structures that make their mark not only on our external conduct but also on our very being. They make us good. We must note an important point here: the virtues never exist in a ready-made or complete form. Their influence is not exercised automatically, in the way that the physical body grows in accordance with the laws that govern it; the virtues need to be cultivated. But they are present in us. They are present as seeds, so to speak, in every person, as a potential that must be developed, often through hard work, mastery of oneself, and sweat. But when they do develop, the garden of our personality puts forth its blossoms, and our human existence is both beautiful and delightful.

An example will make this point clear. Even small children have a very acute sense of justice, and they react strongly to an unjust punishment. I recall very clearly a severe punishment that I felt was just, a punishment that I had genuinely deserved; but I can also recall punishments that were unjust. This delicate sensitivity to questions of injustice and justice is not inculcated in children from the outside; it is present in them as a seed awaiting development, and the virtue of justice comes into being when this sensitivity is cultivated. Education in the virtues always means developing the seeds that are already present in us. If the virtues are to grow, it is essential that we be taught how to educate ourselves: the input cannot come only from others. In order for the sense of justice to develop into a virtue, it is not enough for the child to react strongly when it is the victim of unjust treatment. The child itself must be just and must learn that it is necessary and right to behave justly. Normally, this involves a struggle against oneself and a victory over oneself, because although we possess the seeds of virtue, there is also present in us an inclination to evil.

This is why the seed cannot burgeon without toils and struggles. An education (like the antiauthoritarian praxis) that intends to do without this struggle cannot succeed. Without discipline, we cannot learn any skills or abilities. Athletes need a great deal of self-mastery. They must overcome themselves and practice strict discipline if they are to build up their skills to the point where they can reach outstanding goals.

Where this work of construction is successful and the seeds of the virtues develop, they become the active source of good human conduct. The *Catechism* has a beautiful definition of virtue, which I would like to put alongside that of Saint Thomas: "A virtue is an habitual and firm disposition to do the good."[1] I do not need to make a difficult decision each time, resolving anew to choose and to do the good; rather, virtues incline me to do what is good, and this becomes particularly clear in dramatic situations where I simply do not have the time to reflect on what I ought to do at this moment or to ask anyone else for advice. I have to act at once! And it is here that I can see whether I possess a stable and continuous inclination to do what is good; for in such situations, the good will flow forth from me as from a spring of water, not via my intellect but out of my heart, spontaneous and sure.

Alexander Solzhenitsyn, at the close of *The Gulag Archipelago*, his monumental work about the Soviet concentration camps where he himself was a prisoner for many years, asks: Why was I on the one side rather than the other? Why did I not become an agent of the KGB, a spy, an oppressor? Why did I take the path that led to a concentration camp? He presents an impressive analysis of how this came about: again and again, there were little partings of the ways where he almost unconsciously chose the good rather than the bad, without being aware of the full significance of these little decisions. Solzhenitsyn thought that this inclination to the good, which we call "virtue", came from his education, perhaps from his grandmother. In the difficult and dramatic moments of his life, it allowed him to resist temptation and to choose the

[1] *CCC* 1803.

good. Many of our decisions are not made in a conscious process of choice but are the product of a kind of instinct. If we possess this stable, continuous inclination to the good that we call virtue, our decision making will spontaneously, almost naturally and inherently, go in the right direction.

Let me make two other remarks here. One who has acquired virtue has, so to speak, a natural sense for the good. Saint Thomas uses the example of a judge who is perfectly acquainted with every law that exists and has studied the questions connected with the idea of justice but who is personally an unjust man. In his judicial work, he may reach a correct verdict by following theoretical lines of argument, but this does not make him a just man. Thomas then presents a simple person who cannot find his way around in the thickets of legislation and has not studied moral philosophy but who has a sharp inner sense of justice and who has developed that inclination to the good that we call virtue by doing what is good and just over a long period of time. Such a person may be able to formulate a more correct verdict than the legal professional, precisely because he is sensitive to this whole area and bears in himself the virtue of justice.

Second, we should bear in mind some words of the *Catechism*: the virtues "make possible ease, self-mastery, and joy in leading a morally good life".[2] Just as a good craftsman who understands his métier has a feeling of ease, self-mastery, and joy in his work, so it is with the virtuous person. Someone who has developed his ethical personality does what is good, not with sighs and groans, not gritting his teeth all the time in the effort to overcome himself, but with ease and joy. You can sense the same thing in great artists. I once saw a film about Yehudi Menuhin, the great violinist, who recalled

---

[2] *CCC* 1804.

how hard his childhood was, when he had to practice every day and heard and saw the other children playing outside. Later, however, his playing streamed forth with that radiant ease that is also the characteristic of virtue.

Natural and Divine Virtues

If this is true of every human being, what is its relevance to *Christian* virtue? The pagan philosophers as well as other cultures and religions have the same view of the virtues: they agree that it is only the virtues that make us genuinely human. What then is special about Christian virtue? We believe not only that the human person possesses the seeds of the natural virtues but that in baptism the seeds of the divine virtues were planted in us. It is thus not only the natural virtues that slumber in us and await their development but also the divine life itself: faith, hope, and love. We believe that in baptism, and whenever we receive the sacraments, the divine life is planted in us as a seed that seeks to develop and to bring about a real transformation in us. "If any one is in Christ, he is a new creation" (2 Cor 5:17; cf. Gal 6:15).

Let me try to make this point clearer. The Church Fathers say that the human person—every human person—is created in the image of God, and this is his dignity. Not even the greatest vices or the most terrible crimes can take away from the human person this dignity of being God's image. Genesis tells us that God created the human being "in his image, after his likeness" (cf. 1:26), and the Fathers interpret this to mean that we are all created in the image of God and called to become like him. The image of God is realized in us only to the extent that this image develops and becomes ever more similar to him, so that we resemble God more strongly.

Faith, hope, and love—these three make us like God. The dogmatic teaching of the Church tells us that the divine virtues are a gift, a grace. I cannot get hold of them for myself. All I can do, once I have received them as God's gift, is cultivate them and develop them. Parents know that they can show their children the example of living by faith; they can explain the faith and try to hand it on; but they cannot produce faith. Even in their own children, it remains the gift of Another. And yet we are perfectly correct to use the word "virtues" when we speak of this gift, because they are truly our own. I believe; I hope; I love. God gives them to us in such a way that, like the natural virtues, they become a spring in us. What they generate, however, is not merely ethical human conduct but a life that is linked to God and shares in God. Paul says: "May Christ dwell in your hearts through faith" (cf. Eph 3:17). Let me conclude by drawing your attention to two characteristics of these divine virtues.

The *Catechism* says: "The human virtues are rooted in the theological virtues."[3] Is it not the opposite that seems to be true? Do not the divine virtues need a good, solid human basis? The experience of the Christian life assures us that both are true: in order to lead a Christian life, we need a good human basis, but it is precisely the Christian life that shows us that the human qualities develop by means of faith, hope, and love. We will return in greater detail to this point in the chapter on the gifts of the Holy Spirit.

Faith strengthens reason and helps us to see more clearly. Hope gives us power, the divine power to stand firm under difficult circumstances. Most beautiful of all is love, which is "the bond of perfection" (cf. Col 3:14). We see this above all in the lives of the saints, whose human life came to full

[3] *CCC* 1812.

development precisely thanks to the divine virtues; and this is exemplified most clearly in love itself. Saint Thomas says that there is no virtue whatsoever without love. Prudence without love may be merely a calculating cleverness; justice without love threatens to become unmerciful. Love is the perfect measure of all the human virtues. What would justice, courage, or temperance be without love? This is why Saint Thomas says that love is the "form" of all the virtues. Indeed, it is love that *makes* them virtues, for as Saint Paul says, "it makes all things perfect" (cf. Col 3:14).

7

LETTING ONESELF BE "LED BY THE SPIRIT"

The Gifts of the Spirit

Gracious God, let your grace be powerful in our hearts, so that we can master our own desires and follow the inspirations of your Spirit. We make our prayer through Christ our Lord. Amen.

—Collect for the Third Friday of Lent
(Translated from the German Missal)

The Unknown Holy Spirit

Every year, about ten thousand young people are confirmed in the Archdiocese of Vienna. At each confirmation, the bishop or the priest whom he has charged to administer this sacrament addresses a prayer to the Holy Spirit. He stretches out his hands over those to be confirmed and says:

> All-powerful God, Father of our Lord Jesus Christ,
> by water and the Holy Spirit
> you freed your sons and daughters from sin
> and gave them new life.

Send your Holy Spirit upon them
to be their helper and guide.
Give them the spirit of wisdom and understanding,
the spirit of right judgment and courage,
the spirit of knowledge and reverence.
Fill them with the spirit of wonder and awe in your
    presence.
We ask this through Christ our Lord.

Every time I speak this prayer over the many young people who receive confirmation, I wonder: Do they understand what I am praying over them? Do I myself understand it? Do our young candidates for the sacrament know what the "seven gifts of the Holy Spirit" means? And do I know?

At confirmations, I usually wear a miter that our auxiliary bishop Karl Moser bequeathed to me on his deathbed. It depicts seven flames, and sometimes I take these seven flames as the starting point of my sermon to the candidates. In the present catechesis, I would like to reflect with you on the seven gifts of the Holy Spirit. Do we know what the apostle Paul means when he says: "All who are led by the Spirit of God are sons of God" (Rom 8:14)? Have we been taught about the Holy Spirit, or is he still largely the great unknown in the Church? The apostle Paul once met a group of disciples in Ephesus who had received baptism; but when he asked them: "Did you receive the Holy Spirit when you believed?", they replied: "No, we have never even heard that there is a Holy Spirit" (Acts 19:2). Could the same be said of us Christians today?

The Bible and the Church's life leave no room for doubt: without the Holy Spirit, a Christian life is simply impossible. As the medieval sequence "Veni, Sancte Spiritus" in the Pentecost Mass puts it: "Sine tuo numine, nihil est in

homine, nihil est innoxium." (Traditional English translation: "Where you are not, man has naught, nothing good in
deed or thought, nothing free from taint of ill.")

On the one hand, the Holy Spirit seems to be unknown.
On the other hand, I am sure that many could tell how they
have experienced the Holy Spirit in their lives. They might
be rather reluctant to do so, since the Holy Spirit loves discretion and hiddenness, but it is certain that many have an
explicit inner familiarity with the Holy Spirit, whom the
sequence calls *dulcis hospes animae*, "the soul's sweet guest"
(traditional English translation: "the soul's most welcome
guest"). The Holy Spirit is the guide and comforter of our
life, and many could bear witness to the times in daily existence and in the small things of life when they have experienced his guidance with a particular clarity.

In this series of talks, we are looking at right human conduct and Christian ethics. In this context, we will now ask
what we mean when we speak of the guidance of the Holy
Spirit, and more specifically of his gifts. My intention is to
encourage us all to seek this inner guidance ever more insistently and to entrust ourselves genuinely to the Holy Spirit
in the totality of our lives. It would be wonderful if we quite
spontaneously asked the Holy Spirit for guidance before
every important discussion or piece of work. But perhaps we
already do so without putting this explicitly into words, since
we sense and know in faith that without him we cannot take
the good path.

The Spirit's Guidance—and Our Freedom

"All who are led by the Spirit of God are sons of God",
says Paul (Rom 8:14). They are his sons and daughters in

the sense that they are like the Son of God, since their existence is configured to his. If we ask what it means to be "led by the Spirit", our clearest answer is found in Jesus himself. Throughout his life, we see him as one who allows the Spirit to lead him in every matter. Clearly, Paul too has experienced powerfully that to allow oneself to be led by the Spirit means to become truly free. In his Second Letter to the Corinthians, he writes: "Where the Spirit of the Lord is, there is freedom" (3:17). It follows that where the Spirit of the Lord is not at work, there is slavery. But how is this possible? If I am led by the Spirit, how can this be freedom? For surely, if I allow someone else to lead me, I am not free. Does not freedom mean first and foremost self-determination, autonomy? If someone else leads me, it is he who determines everything, and this is heteronomy. But what if I lead myself? Surely it is our task to lead our own lives, assuming personal responsibility for what we do. But do I really succeed in taking control of my own life? Is it not rather the case that I am often led by my passions? The apostle Paul speaks of this in a dramatic text. He observes that he is not at all led by his own self (Rom 7:15–19):

> I do not understand my own actions. For I do not do what I want, but I do the very thing I hate. Now if I do what I do not want, I agree that the law is good. So then it is no longer I that do it, but sin which dwells within me. For I know that nothing good dwells within me, that is, in my flesh. I can will what is right, but I cannot do it. For I do not do the good I want, but the evil I do not want is what I do.

And he goes on to exclaim:

> Wretched man that I am! Who will deliver me from this body of death? (7:24)

Paul's experience of this inner laceration is indeed dramatic. He wants to take charge of his own life, but he observes that there is something else in him that leads him, although he does not want to be led by this. We may call this "evil" or "sin"; he speaks of "the flesh" or "another law" (7:23). But he concludes with a great upsurge of emotion straight from the heart: "Thanks be to God through Jesus Christ our Lord! So then, I of myself serve the law of God with my mind, but with my flesh I serve the law of sin" (7:25). "Thanks be to God through Jesus Christ", who has set him free. This experience makes Paul certain that he is free *only* when the Holy Spirit of Jesus guides his life. He knows that in the innermost depths of his being, it is not the law of sin or the law of evil but the Holy Spirit who must take control. He has to hand over the rudder of his life to the Holy Spirit, for only then will he be free. Until the Holy Spirit becomes our helmsman, we are driven about—even when we think that we are free. For when we are driven by our passions, we are slaves.

In the previous catechesis we discussed the virtues, which are meant to make it possible for us to guide our lives ourselves and to be inherently inclined to direct our lives to a good end. The virtues are attitudes that make us ready and willing to do what is good, dispositions of the personality that lead us to do what is right with a certain spontaneity, as something almost natural, something we can take for granted. One who has acquired the virtue of kindliness, perhaps at the cost of repeated struggles and renewed endeavors, will not lose it so easily. It does not entail completely fresh toil, since it has become second nature to him. Exactly the same is true of patience, courage, temperance, or justice. We apply the word "virtue" to qualities that have genuinely become our own and can to some extent be taken for granted, so that an inner sensitivity leads us to do what is right precisely in situations where there is little time for reflection and we must act quickly. Such circumstances show our true natures! And they will teach us that the virtues make it easy for us to do spontaneously what is right. As Saint Thomas says: "A virtue is that which makes the person who possesses it good."

The great ethical masters—Plato, Aristotle, and Socrates in his own way—held that we can achieve this uprightness and become just and good through practice, discipline, and the effort of the will. We have seen that the apostle Paul takes a different view. He sees human life in altogether more dramatic terms. Perhaps because he has drawn closer to God thanks to his faith, he sees more clearly how much still needs to be purified in his innermost being, in his heart, in his life as a whole. Much is not yet upright. He discovers in himself this other law that continually leads him astray, and he draws the conclusion that without the help of God, without the Holy Spirit, the human person cannot be upright. Without the merciful presence of the Spirit, we have "nothing good in deed or thought". And it is here that the doctrine of the seven gifts of the Holy Spirit has its starting point.

There Is No Christian Life without the Holy Spirit

Saint Thomas was convinced that we cannot attain salvation without the seven gifts of the Holy Spirit. Without the Spirit's guidance, the human person cannot achieve eternal happiness, no matter how titanic his endeavors might be. We find the origin of the doctrine of the seven gifts of the Holy Spirit in a passage in the prophet Isaiah, when God promises the Messiah, who will be born of the family of David (11:1–2):

There shall come forth a shoot from the stump of Jesse,
and a branch shall grow out of his roots.
And the Spirit of the LORD shall rest upon him,
the spirit of wisdom and understanding,
the spirit of counsel and might,
the spirit of knowledge and the fear of the LORD.

This text is the root on which all later tradition has medi-
tated. In the Greek and Latin translations, a seventh gift was
added to the six in the original Hebrew text: "the fear of the
Lord" was divided into "fear of the Lord" and "piety".

Jesus himself refers to a similar text from the prophet Isaiah
when he unrolls the book of Scripture in the synagogue in
Nazareth and reads aloud the following words: "The Spirit
of the Lord GOD is upon me, because the LORD has anointed
me" (Is 61:1; Lk 4:18). The Gospels, especially that of Luke,
repeatedly emphasize that Jesus performs every action in the
Holy Spirit. The Spirit drives him out into the wilderness
and leads him back to Galilee. At the various stages in Jesus'
life, we are told that the Spirit leads him (Lk 1:15, 17; 3:22;
4:1, 14; 10:21). And Jesus wants his disciples to be filled with
the Spirit (Lk 11:13; 12:12). According to John, the first
thing Jesus does after the Resurrection is to breathe on them
with the words: "Receive the Holy Spirit" (Jn 20:22). The
entire history of the early Church is an intense experience
of being led by the Holy Spirit. The Christian life is always
a life in the Holy Spirit, as the whole of Christian tradition
has attested from the earliest days until the *Catechism of the
Catholic Church*, whose third part (dealing with morality) has
the subsection "Man's Vocation: Life in the Spirit". Christian
living is living in the Holy Spirit. The *Catechism* says that its
teaching about the ten commandments of the Christian life
"should be *a catechesis of the Holy Spirit*, the interior Master

of life according to Christ, a gentle guest and friend who inspires, guides, corrects, and strengthens this life".[1]

Is this truly so in our lives? How far are we aware that the Christian life in keeping with the commandments of God is a life in the Holy Spirit? Saint Thomas Aquinas says that although all the virtues are important, they do not lead to life without the Holy Spirit. He explicitly affirms that the gifts of the Holy Spirit are necessary for salvation. They are not something for an elite consisting of a few specially chosen "mystical" souls; they are necessary for everyone's salvation. Without them, no one arrives at the goal of eternal life. And this means quite simply that our own endeavors do not suffice for a successful life. We can no doubt achieve many things through the hard work of our will and our reason, but that is not how life reaches its goal.

How Does the Holy Spirit Lead Us?

Why are the gifts of the Holy Spirit so essential for life and salvation that we cannot be saved without them? How does one perceive the presence of these gifts? Are there signs that help me to assess whether the Holy Spirit is at work in my life and I am letting him lead me?

Why is it impossible to do without the gifts of the Holy Spirit? Let me return to the subject of the virtues. The virtues—attitudes that we acquire and that are given to us— incline us to do good. I do not have to make a fresh decision in favor of the good again and again in one or another sphere of my life; I do so thanks to an attitude that has genuinely become my own. If all I seek here is a practical orientation

[1] *CCC* 1697.

in my life, this might seem to suffice; but a closer look shows that life as a whole cannot succeed in this way. It is impossible for me to know many individual details that are necessary to provide an orientation in my life. The antenna of my reason, my prudence, or my insights is not powerful enough to map out reality for me in such a way that I will arrive safely at my goal.

There is a yet more radical reason why my own reason and virtues are insufficient. In the Sermon on the Mount and in other passages, Jesus speaks of a righteousness that "exceeds that of the scribes and Pharisees" (Mt 5:20). He is not saying that the righteousness of the scribes and Pharisees is something bad; but it is inadequate. Jesus is saying: If all you have is this righteousness—a rational, human righteousness—then you will never enter the kingdom of heaven. A greater righteousness is needed, something more than decency and a good intention, for although these are certainly good, they do not go far enough.

The eight beatitudes in the Sermon on the Mount (Mt 5:3–12) speak of this righteousness, which is greater than what we customarily think of as decent human behavior. Jesus tells us that if our righteousness is not greater than loving our neighbor and hating our enemy, then we cannot enter the kingdom of heaven (5:43–48). He speaks of reconciliation (5:23–26). An example of the greater righteousness is turning the other cheek when someone strikes us (5:39). But can we do this on our own? How impossible it is to love one's enemies! And yet Jesus says that if we do not love them, there is no admittance for us to the kingdom of heaven (5:46–48; Lk 6:32–36). He requires that we work in secret: we are not to give alms with the intention of being seen by others, and we are not to make a public exhibition of our pious deeds (Mt 6:2–4). It is irrelevant what other people might say about us; all that matters is that "your Father who sees in secret will reward you" (6:4, 6, 18). *That* is important! And all this belongs to the greater righteousness. Similarly, the lilies of the field and the birds of the air should be models for us, since they are confident that God will care for them (6:26–31). Are we able to entrust our lives so radically to divine providence?

Everything in the Sermon on the Mount—what Jesus calls the greater righteousness—is necessary if we are to reach the kingdom of heaven. There are no cut-rate entry tickets. Even a brief reflection shows that more is involved here than natural virtues. Jesus himself says that one who lives according to the Sermon on the Mount has not built his house on sand (Mt 7:24–27). The "house" of his life will not be torn down by storm and flood. Only those who build the house of their lives on Christ the Rock will enter into life. And this can succeed only if we allow our life to be guided by the Spirit of God.

Recognizing the Gifts of the Spirit

The greater righteousness remains inaccessible even if we allow ourselves to be guided by our own good instincts. It succeeds only when the instinct of the Holy Spirit guides us and God himself moves us. The gifts of the Holy Spirit are like the virtues in that they too incline us to do what is good—but not with our own power. The gifts of the Holy Spirit function in such a way that the Spirit himself inclines us to things that go beyond merely human goodness and righteousness.

Let me make this clearer by means of an example. In 1215 Saint Dominic began to gather his first brethren. Initially, there were no more than sixteen of them. Then Dominic made a completely crazy decision. In 1217, after living for one year with the handful of these first brethren, he sent them in groups to various cities throughout Europe and charged them to preach the Gospel and found monasteries. He sent them to Madrid, Paris, Bologna, and Rome; one group remained in Toulouse. Humanly speaking, this was sheer madness. What could be more imprudent than to send out such a small flock of brethren after so short a time? But Dominic acted here in a way that went beyond human prudence: clearly, he had received a powerful inspiration from the Holy Spirit and was convinced that he had to act in this way. God was prompting him, and Dominic had to obey.

But how are we to discern whether an action is madness or an inspiration from the Spirit of God? The mere fact that other people call something we do crazy does not mean that the Holy Spirit is moving us to act! In this instance, we can at any rate say that Dominic was successful, or that his brethren were of such good quality that they succeeded in this hazardous undertaking. They did in fact found monastic communities in many places, and new recruits joined the order very soon, so that it expanded with extraordinary speed. The outcome of Dominic's action was not a catastrophe but a success.

There are countless similar examples in the biographies of the saints. Teresa of Avila could certainly not have carried through her monastic reform without possessing a quality that went beyond merely human prudence (though without being simply mad!). But not everyone who puts his trust in divine providence and takes huge financial risks is necessarily following an instinct of the Holy Spirit; this may be merely a case of presumptuous imprudence. How then do we discern whether the Holy Spirit is prompting us to go beyond the normal measure or whether we are being led

astray by imprudence and a presumptuous overestimation of
our own abilities?

Do we not see in every Christian life, even in small matters, the continual invitation to something greater than the
normal human measure, to take steps that others may consider irrational yet that possess a deeper rationality, namely,
the rationality of the Holy Spirit? For example, a person goes
against all apparent reason and human prudence by forgiving
his spouse and making a fresh start possible. And I recently
heard of a man who chose not to do something that is common and taken for granted in today's society. It was suggested
to him that he should obtain a medical recommendation that
would allow him to take a well-paid early retirement; but
since this useful recommendation would have been a lie, his
Christian conviction led him to resolve not to cheat society.
This man preferred to earn less money and to leave work at a
later date with a smaller pension—and according to the customary logic of our world, such an action is crazy. But does
not one who acts in this way demonstrate that gift of strength
that the Holy Spirit gives us?

Let us return to Saint Dominic. How can one determine
whether such actions are the fruit of a frivolous irresponsibil-
ity or the fruit of an inspiration of the Holy Spirit? Despite
objections and resistance, Saint Dominic himself was convinced that he was moved by the Spirit. It seems clear that if
we are to follow the Holy Spirit in this way, we need antennae that can perceive the inspirations that he gives us. A spiritual master once offered a vivid definition of the gifts of the
Holy Spirit, which I have made my own: they are antennae
that allow us to receive the words the Holy Spirit addresses to
us. Without such antennae—or without a global positioning
system like that in an automobile, if the technically minded
prefer an even more modern image—the Holy Spirit cannot

guide us. There is of course an essential difference between the GPS in my car and the gifts of the Holy Spirit, namely, the latter do not guide us from the outside but from within. They permit us to be led by the Holy Spirit from the heart, from our innermost being. This is not heteronomous but rather the fruit of an innermost sensitivity. This is why we speak of the *gifts* of the Holy Spirit: just as the virtues become our own, so too the gifts of the Holy Spirit are bestowed on us to become our own. They take the form of a sensitivity in us, an instinct for the working of the Holy Spirit. And the surest sign that an internal inspiration comes from him is the joy and peace that it brings.

It is only thus that we can explain one of the fundamental experiences of Christianity, namely, that so many simple people who have never studied theology at a university nevertheless have a sure feeling for the inspiration of the Holy Spirit and truly perform actions that are in accordance with the greater righteousness. It is marvelous to witness the working of the Holy Spirit in the lives of people who are led by him to take admirable steps that transcend the normal measure—steps of mercy, of kindness, of reconciliation, of wisdom, and also of strength.

Another image the spiritual masters like to employ when they explain the difference between the virtues and the gifts of the Holy Spirit is that of a rowboat. If you wish to cross the great ocean in a rowboat, you have no easy task! It is not absolutely impossible, but it is exceedingly difficult: you yourself must be very strong, and there must be no vigorous headwind. But when you hoist a sail in your boat and the wind puffs out this sail, you can travel easily and quickly to the far shore. The spiritual masters say that this is how things are with the gifts of the Holy Spirit. As long as I proceed by my own efforts, I am like one who rows—I do make some progress, but the work is arduous. But if I possess the gifts of the Spirit, the boat of my life has hoisted its sail and the wind of the Holy Spirit blows on it, so that the boat makes easy progress. Such a life will certainly have the radiance, joyfulness, and ease that are always the signs of the Holy Spirit.

Each of these seven gifts strengthens our own natural gifts. Wisdom, understanding, knowledge, fortitude, the fear of God, counsel, piety—we all know people in whom we can observe at least something of each of these gifts. This plurality is fundamentally a unity, for all of this is love: love is that gift of the Spirit that forms the synthesis of all the others. If then we want to summarize the present catechesis, we can say that the surest sign that we are guided by the Spirit of God is when we let ourselves be guided by love. But we need the antennae! The Spirit can inspire us only if we are able to receive his inspirations. This is why we continually pray for the seven gifts of the Holy Spirit. When we pray for the seven gifts of the Holy Spirit for those who are about to receive the sacrament of confirmation, we pray that in some way, thanks to this prayer and to the sacrament, antennae may be activated for an entire life. We do not know to what extent the candidates will use them or how they will develop. These antennae are present in each one of us from baptism onward. And this is why we pray for the gifts of the Holy Spirit in our own lives too.

8

SIN

Turning One's Back on God

Lord Jesus Christ, on the evening of Easter Sunday, you stood in the midst of your disciples and said: "Peace be with you!" We pray therefore, O Victor over sin and death: do not look on our sins but on the faith of your Church, and grant us according to your will unity and peace. Who live and reign forever and ever. Amen.

Who Still Speaks of Sin Nowadays?

When we discuss the foundations of ethical living, we cannot avoid speaking of a reality that we so frequently encounter, namely, sin. When someone unaccustomed to our liturgical language attends Mass, he may be struck by how often sin is mentioned. At the beginning of the service, we say: "I confess ... that I have greatly sinned." This theme recurs again and again until the prayer before the sign of peace: "Look not on our sins, but on the faith of your Church." Even in the Gloria, a song in praise of God's glory, we say, "Lamb of God, ... you take away the sins of the world," and this expression is echoed later, first in the threefold Agnus Dei—"Lamb of God, you take away the sins of the world"—and then when the priest invites those present to receive communion: "Behold the Lamb of God, behold him who takes away the sins of the world." Sin is also mentioned in the silent prayers of the priest. For example, after the Gospel has been read, the priest or deacon prays: "Through the words of the Gospel may our sins be wiped away." When the priest washes his hands, he prays: "Wash me, O Lord, from my iniquity and cleanse me from my sin" (cf. Ps 51:2). Before communion, he prays silently in his own name and in that of all the believers who will receive the sacrament: "Free me by this, your most holy Body and Blood, from all my sins and from every evil."

An external observer might have the impression that the Catholic Church is obsessed with sin—for surely so much repetition of one theme must amount to an "obsession". Is it not somewhat morbid to go on and on about sin? Are Christians people who smell out sin everywhere and see everything in the negative light of sin? Is this not symptomatic of an attitude that makes both other people and one's own self sick? Christianity is often accused of making people neurotic, precisely because of this continual emphasis on sin.

Let us begin our discussion by affirming that sin is one of the central words of our faith and that it therefore cannot simply be eliminated. Even if the word itself has become foreign to us, there is no other that can take its place. Let us look at the words of consecration that the priest pronounces over the wine in the name of Jesus. He says: "This is the chalice of my Blood, the Blood of the new and eternal covenant, which will be poured out for you and for many *for the forgiveness of sins.*"[1] This means that the reason Jesus died was to bring

---

[1] Emphasis added.

about the forgiveness of sins. Indeed, the evangelist Matthew explains the name "Jesus" on the basis of the mission that is to determine the whole of Jesus' life: "You shall call his name Jesus, for he will save his people from their sins" (Mt 1:21). Jesus came to earth and died so that sins might be forgiven. At the end of the creed, we solemnly proclaim that we believe in "the forgiveness of sins". But if we believe in their forgiveness, then we also believe that sins exist.

In the doctrine of faith, therefore, the word "sin" has an importance that is not reflected in the banalities of everyday speech. In German, it is common to use the word for sin to designate crimes—for example, offenses against the current traffic or construction or environmental regulations. In Austria, when something is particularly expensive, people call it "sinfully dear". Both in German and in English, however, the word "sin" mostly occurs in matters concerning the sixth commandment. "Can it be a sin to love?" The question is often heard nowadays; but it narrows down both "sin" and "love" to the sexual sphere alone.

What Is Sin?

The first point about which we must be clear is that something more than intellectual reflection is needed if we are to grasp the significance of the word and of the reality of sin. This is not primarily a matter for academic theology. There is another kind of insight and knowledge, seated not in the understanding but in the heart, and it is there that we comprehend what sin is.

Before we look at this in greater detail, let us begin with the superficial examples I have mentioned. Perhaps they do preserve a faded recollection of what sin actually is. The

German expressions "traffic sins", "building sins", and "environmental sins" designate an infringement of the regulations governing traffic, buildings, or environmental pollution, and this points us in the right direction, for sin always involves an infringement of the order of things. At the same time, it is obvious that not every infringement of every regulation counts as sin. Even in this superficial use of language, the word is reserved for especially grave matters: if someone parks badly, we might perhaps say that he is not a good driver, but we would not call this a "traffic sin" in German.

If the word "sin" is to be justified even in this superficial use of language, there must be something in addition to the offense against a regulation; there must be an element of *intention*. We can go even further and say that there must be an element of *malice* involved. This does not mean that the perpetrator must be aware of this at the precise moment when he is breaking the rules; but this is how others experience it, and he himself can become painfully aware later on that what he did was not merely a slight bending of the regulations. Something worse was involved. And suddenly, one is aware of the fact that one has incurred guilt.

As I thought about these questions, I recalled a fellow student in high school who was badly spoiled. His parents were wealthy, and he was their only child. His parents often left him alone, and he began to borrow their car without permission when he was only about fifteen or sixteen and to race at high speeds around the neighborhood. I remember very well taking him to task when he boasted of this in class—because I knew that my mother had driven to work that day along the very same road. I was furious and asked him: "Do you know what you're doing? Don't you know you are putting other people's lives at risk?" A few months later, he crashed into a tree at ninety miles an hour. He was sixteen years old, and three others were in the car with him, all under eighteen; and all four died.

When we speak in German of "environmental sins", we do not simply mean things that happen by chance or unintentionally. We mean things like the tragic interplay of various economic and political interests that leads to the unchecked devastation of the rain forests. I will return later to this question of the links between various elements, which today are often called the "structures of sin".

The Tremendous Significance of Sin

We have seen that even the superficial way in which we speak of sin in our everyday language includes the element of deliberate intention or malice, at least in such a way that this can later be discovered when the conscience awakens. This prompts the question whether this use of the term "sin" in nonecclesiastical contexts is in fact a remnant of religious language. Is this merely an outdated theatrical prop of Christianity that has lingered on in secular society, or does this use of "sin" express a deeper sensitivity, a faded notion of what sin truly is?

Let us consult the *Catechism*, which offers two definitions of sin. At first sight, these are contradictory. In *CCC* 1849, we read: "Sin is an offense against reason, truth, and right conscience." In *CCC* 1850, we are then told: "Sin is an offense against God." Does this not amount to an antithesis? At the very least, objections can be made to these two definitions.

Is an offense against reason ipso facto sin? Is not sin always connected with God, with a religious context? This is why many people assert that one ought not to speak of sin in the sphere of reason but perhaps only of guilt. Sin is an explicitly religious word, while guilt exists also in the nonreligious sphere. Is not sin out of place in the profane, secular realm? One can incur guilt there, but can one sin? When the second definition asserts that sin is an offense against God, some people reply: "But one cannot 'offend' God, who is infinitely exalted above anything that *we* can do. We cannot wound him." And so we can ask: Is not sin basically an erroneous concept, one we ought really to abandon? In the human sphere, we should speak of guilt; and it is completely impossible to offend God. Ought not the word "sin" be deposited in the museum of religious theatrical props?

There is a famous medieval dialogue between an abbot and his disciple, who is also a monk, about the question *Cur Deus homo?* "Why did God become man?" Why did God send his Son to become a human being? What could have moved God to send his Son into this world? At one point in this lengthy dialogue between the abbot and his monastic pupil, the conversation breaks down. Then the abbot, Saint Anselm of Canterbury, says to his disciple Boso: "You have not yet considered the tremendous weight that sin has."[2] A completely different move is required if we are to become conscious of the "weight" of sin, and we will now attempt to make this move with our heart and with our faith. Let us try to keep before our eyes what the faith says, even if we cannot always *feel* the truth of what it teaches. In faith, we assert that the significance of sin is so tremendous that it cost God his life. The Son of God died because of our sins. We discern the true weight of sin only when we see the ransom that God paid because of it.

At the beginning of this catechesis, I asked why we speak so often of sin during the Mass. Perhaps the answer is clearer

---

[2] *Cur Deus homo?* 1.21.

now: it is because the death and Resurrection of Jesus are celebrated precisely in the Eucharist. As the Second Vatican Council says, whenever we celebrate this sacrifice, "the work of our redemption is accomplished".[3] The work of redemption becomes a present reality every time the Eucharist is celebrated, and this reveals how much our sin cost God.

We can put this somewhat differently: it is only when we look to the Eucharist, to the cross, to the death and Resurrection of Jesus, that sin is revealed to us. Perhaps this explains why Christianity speaks so much about sin: it is in fact only through Christ that sin is truly revealed. Before he came, one could tell oneself that things were not really *so* bad; at any rate, the full dimensions of the reality called sin were not yet known. It is only the cross that discloses the full weight of sin. *My* sin cost God his life—the sin of us all, the sin of the world, the whole weight of sin that the Lamb of God took upon himself.

God's Love and Our Sin

It is only when we encounter the full extent of God's forgiving love in the cross that we grasp the extent and weight of our sin. This is why we both can and indeed must say that only Christ has revealed the full reality of sin. Before he came, much remained veiled. But when Jesus breathed out the Spirit on the cross, then breathed him into the disciples on Easter and poured him out upon them at Pentecost, the full dimensions of sin were revealed. Jesus himself announced that this would happen, when he spoke to the apostles at the

---

[3] Constitution on the Sacred Liturgy, *Sacrosanctum Concilium*, 2, quoting the secret of the ninth Sunday after Pentecost, Holy See website, www.vatican.va.

Last Supper. Three times he spoke of the Spirit who was to come, and the third time, he said that the Spirit, the Counselor whom he would send, "will convince the world concerning sin" (Jn 16:7ff.). This means that it is only the Holy Spirit who makes us aware of the tremendous significance of sin. Only where grace and forgiveness are given superabundantly can the reality of sin be disclosed.

A Family Example

A simple human experience will show what I mean. A child who is unloved and knows he is not accepted will find it very difficult to go to his parents when he has done something wrong and to own up. His tactics may vary—he will deny all guilt, play for time, hide defiantly, assert his innocence, or perhaps throw the blame on others—but one thing is certain: he will not admit any guilt. A child who knows himself to be loved and lives in the inner certainty that he is accepted may also find it difficult to admit guilt. But this particular block will not exist. He knows that if he goes to his mother or father and admits to having done something wrong, he will not be rejected. He knows that his parents will not turn their backs on him. In one sense, we might almost say that a child who grows up experiencing rejection is *obliged* for reasons of psychological health not to admit any guilt, because that would be tantamount to psychological suicide. A child who is always kept dangling—"If you are good, I will love you, and if you are not good, I will not love you"—will not be certain whether his parents love him, and such a child will not be able to feel confident enough to admit his guilt. But a child who knows himself secure in his parents' love can tell them openly about his guilt. He will meet not rejection but forgiveness.

Experience shows us something that is truly astonishing: it is precisely in this experience of being accepted that we become conscious of the depth of our guilt. If I know that I am truly loved by my parents, I suffer because of my guilt, since I know that I have offended against love. The more deeply I am accepted, the greater my consciousness of my own guilt. This may sound surprising, but it is precisely when the parents do not hurl accusations at the child and reproach him—"Why did you do that?"—but instead come to meet him with love, that a space opens up in which the child can recognize and declare what he has done wrong. It is painful to hurt those whom I love and who I know love me, and this makes possible the repentance that heals.

Encountering God's Love

Is not this the core of the good news? The apostle John tells us: "He loved us first" (cf. 1 Jn 4:19). God does not love us because we are well behaved; rather, it is because God loves us that we can dare to recognize how wretched we are and how much in us is sin. It is only in the light of this love that we can discern how much weight sin has, for otherwise we would have to be like the child who keeps on stalling and blaming others, since his fear of rejection is so great that he can never own up to anything. There is surely no passage in the Gospels that expresses this truth more profoundly than Jesus' words to the woman who had been caught in adultery: "Neither do I condemn you; go, and do not sin again" (Jn 8:11). Insight into one's sin is possible only when one knows that one is not condemned, and this is why grace always has the priority vis-à-vis sin.

Peter experiences grace in this way when he encounters the gaze of Jesus (Lk 22:61). We may not have seen the face

of Jesus, but we believe that he sees us, and in faith we have
seen him. There is no trace of condemnation in his eyes, only
a love that hastens to meet us, welcoming us and giving us
everything. And this is why Peter weeps bitterly. After deny-
ing the Lord three times on the night when Jesus was arrested
and tried, he encountered his gaze. I believe that this revealed
to him the whole depth and horror of his sin; but at the same
time, the eyes of Jesus showed Peter that he was forgiven. Sin
can be truly perceived only to the extent that we recognize
the presence of forgiveness. The one who encounters this
love can begin to appreciate the terrible significance of sin,
namely, the fact that sin says no to this love—it is not merely
the infringement of some rule. Saint Francis said: "Because
Love is not loved." My pain is caused by the realization that
I have failed to love Love.

Does this mean that sin is "an offense against God"? Let
us recall the words of the *Catechism*: "Sin is an offense against
God: '*Against you, you alone*, have I sinned, and done that
which is evil in your sight' [Ps 51:4]. Sin sets itself against
God's love for us and turns our hearts away from it.... Sin is
thus 'love of oneself even to contempt of God'."[4] But if sin is
primarily an offense against God, in the sense that it says no to
his love, how then is it also an offense against reason? What
does all this have to do with reason? I have already mentioned Saint Anselm. In his conversation with his pupil Boso,
he reflects at length on this question and finally says: Everything that offends against the good order established by God
also offends against reason, since it is our reason that permits
us to recognize (at least in a fragmentary manner) the good
of the order of God, the order of creation, and the order of

---

[4] *CCC* 1850; the last words are a quotation from Augustine, *City of God*
14.28. Emphasis added.

human life in society. Our reason often speaks plainly enough about all this. Any offense against reason is an offense against God's good ordering, which reason shows us.

In this sense, one may certainly say that a "sin against the environment" is a sin against God, because it involves disregard for the order of creation, which expresses his will. One who despises the work of God offends against his will and hence against his love: he is offending God. The Bible tells us that God looks on the human person as "the apple of his eye" (Ps 17:8; Zech 2:8), the most precious of all creatures on earth. And this is why the Bible also attests that some actions, such as the exploitation of the poor, are "sins that cry to heaven".[5] Since God protects human beings, an offense against the order of human life in society is also an offense against God. Sin therefore is always contrary to reason *and* an offense against God.

Venial and Mortal Sins

We have attempted to reflect on the terrible significance of sin. But are all sins equally weighty? Are they all on the same level? Are there not some sins that just happen? And do these have the same weight as grave sins? I would like to conclude by saying something about this distinction between grave sins and venial sins and then about the mysterious words of Jesus about the "sin against the Holy Spirit".

In the individual's life of faith, an apparently tiny sin can in fact have an enormous weight. In a moment of disgust, I can become aware of the whole weight of sin that is in me. Nevertheless, we do make a distinction between venial and

[5] *CCC* 1867; Ex 22:20–22; Deut 24:14–15.

mortal sins. The *Catechism* says: *"Mortal sin* destroys charity in the heart of man by a grave violation of God's law."[6] It ruptures the existential link to God and interrupts our path toward him. In comparison, a venial sin is a brief detour, not a fundamental abandoning of the path that leads to God.

But does mortal sin really exist? It is well known that earlier generations were all too ready to apply this term to many actions; today, the danger is that we are unwilling to apply this term to virtually anything at all. Can we then genuinely speak of mortal sin today? The Church's teaching declares that a mortal sin entails three elements. First of all, it must be a truly serious action; traditionally, the examples given are murder, large-scale theft, adultery, blasphemy of God, apostasy from the faith. This is called *grave matter*. Second, there must be the *full knowledge* that this action truly is serious. Even more difficult is the third point, the *full consent*, in other words, the assent of a completely free will.[7] Does it in fact happen that we commit such a sin, in full knowledge that it is so serious that it removes us from the sphere of the love of God, with full consent and full clarity? This is certainly possible. "Mortal sin is a radical possibility of human freedom, as is love itself."[8]

The *Catechism* also affirms that mortal sins can proceed from "hardness of heart".[9] When we look at the Gospel, the really terrifying sins are not so much the grave actions committed consciously and deliberately but the sins of omission, the terrible neglect: the rich man lives in luxury and no longer sees Lazarus at his gate (Lk 16:19–31). Blindness of heart is much more serious than one single evil deed. In Matthew's

[6] *CCC* 1855.
[7] *CCC* 1858–59.
[8] *CCC* 1861.
[9] *CCC* 1859; cf. Mk 3:5–6.

Gospel, the Lord tells us that he will say at the last judgment: "I was sick and you did not visit me, I was poor and you did not help me, I was naked and you did not clothe me.... As you did it not to one of the least of these brothers of mine, you did it not to me" (cf. Mt 25:42–45). Sins of omission can be very grave. The danger is that we no longer notice them, since our heart has become so hard.

If we are too easygoing about our venial sins, this too can lead to hardness of heart. Augustine says: "You may think them harmless when you weigh them one by one; but tremble, when you count up their total!"[10] The individual instance may be harmless, a small lack of kindness, but many little acts like this can make my heart hard. This is why the priest prays so insistently before communion: "Never let me be parted from you." Each one of us must be aware of this risk—it exists in my life too.

The question of the sin against the Holy Spirit is decisive here. Jesus says that every sin and blasphemy will be forgiven, even blasphemy against the Son of Man, "but whoever blasphemes against the Holy Spirit never has forgiveness" (Mk 3:29). Saint Catherine of Siena says that there is only one sin that God cannot forgive, namely, the belief that our sins are greater than his mercy and that his mercy is insufficient for my sins. The *Catechism* makes the same point when it says that God's hands are tied when "anyone ... deliberately refuses to accept his mercy by repenting".[11] Whether a sin is mortal or venial, the essential quality is repentance, the boundless confidence in the mercy of God.

Let me return to my starting point. What reveals sin to us? It is only the mercy of God, only Jesus, who truly reveals why

---

[10] *Commentary on 1 John* 1.6.
[11] *CCC* 1864; cf. John Paul II, *Dominum Vivificantem*, 46.

sin has such a weight. And it is only when we recognize this that we realize that sin is not banal. I close with some words from the First Letter of John, the disciple who truly knew the greatness of the Lord's love (1:8–9): "If we say we have no sin, we deceive ourselves, and the truth is not in us. If we confess our sins, he is faithful and just, and will forgive our sins and cleanse us from all unrighteousness."

9

GRACE

God's Gift to Us

*God our Father, by the waters of baptism you give new life to
the faithful. May we not succumb to the influence of evil but
remain true to your gift of life. We make our prayer through
Christ our Lord. Amen.*

—Collect for Third Saturday of Easter
(Translated from the German Missal)

In Eastertide, we hear a lot about grace. The prayers at Mass
speak of "your gift of grace" or "the life of grace". One prayer
asks for "the grace of faith", while another prays: "Preserve
your grace in us." Yet another asks: "In the Easter mystery,
you have opened up for us the spring of grace. Help us to
make progress in doing good, so that the paschal grace may
always be the source of our life." But what is grace? What
does this word mean? In the present catechesis, we will ask
what the Church teaches on this point, and we will then
examine how grace works and manifests itself in our lives.
The first question is therefore: Is it possible to observe grace?
Can one recognize its presence? Do we experience grace?

When God Gives Something of His Own Self

Let me begin with some words of Saint Paul: "Where sin increased, grace abounded all the more" (Rom 5:20). The previous catechesis spoke of the reality of sin, and we have seen that grace is the presupposition that makes it possible to recognize sin. If a child knows that he is not accepted and feels rejected, he will find it difficult to admit some mistake—if he has told a lie, for example, or broken something. A child who knows he is not accepted will throw the blame on others and make excuses for himself. He cannot recognize and confess his guilt because he has no space to do so. This child lacks the trust that is necessary if one is to acknowledge one's guilt and own up to what one has done. A simple human experience teaches that I can admit my mistakes only in a situation where I know that I am accepted; and this is confirmed and taken to a deeper level in the sphere of faith. Because I know in faith that God loves me, I do not have to be crushed by my guilt: I can *recognize* it and *confess* it. I can accept it as *my* guilt, repent, and make a new start. And this confirms what the apostle says: grace is always greater than guilt. It is only in the light of grace that I become aware of the depth of my guilt.

When I read the biographies of the saints, I am continually astonished by the strength of their consciousness of guilt or sin. The great Catherine of Siena, at the end of her life, said that she was guilty of all the evils in the world. In terms of our normal everyday understanding of things, this is an exorbitant exaggeration, but she held this conviction because she had recognized more profoundly than most people the incomprehensible greatness, breadth, and depth of the love of God. In the presence of this love, she became truly aware of her own wretchedness, and so she could speak as she did.

But what then is grace? The term does still occur in our ordinary everyday speech, but it has become something of a foreign word to us. Yet Scripture is full of the word "grace" and even fuller of the reality that it designates. The word occurs 155 times in the New Testament.

Let me tell a story that illustrates what grace is. These events took place in the twentieth century and left a deep impression on me, since this story was the key that allowed me to understand what grace means. It was told to me by Nicholas Rajevsky, an old Russian whom I met in Vienna in 1968 when I was a young Dominican, twenty-three years old. He was working at that time for a French cultural institute. He came from an old aristocratic family in Russia, the dynasty of the Rajevsky princes, and had been a page at the imperial court in his youth. After the Russian Revolution in 1917, he fled under dramatic circumstances and came to France, where he enlisted in the Foreign Legion and became an officer. The story I shall now relate took place in the Foreign Legion. One of his legionnaires was a German whom he described as "a real brute", a cruel and brutal man who was impossible to like. This foreign legionnaire was wounded so severely in a battle that he had only a short time to live, and he asked his officer, Nicholas Rajevsky, to come to see him. Rajevsky went unwillingly, since he had never heard anything good from the lips of this man, but to his amazement, the gravely wounded man addressed him in very courteous and precise words: "Do you believe that God can give me something of his own self?" The young Russian officer, who was not particularly religious, was surprised at this question and asked him: "What do you mean?" The wounded man replied: "If I die now and come before God with all the dirt of my life, the saints will point their fingers at me. I will be ashamed, and I will not be able to enter heaven. But if God gives me something of his own self, the saints will not be able to say anything against me." Nicholas Rajevsky, who at that date was about as old as I was when he told me the story, did not know exactly what to say. He told the German soldier: "God will certainly give you something of his own self." And then the legionnaire died.

I believe that these words indicate exactly what is involved in grace: *If God gives me something of his own self . . .* That is a very precise definition. I can appear before God only if he gives me something of his own self, for only then can I be acceptable in the eyes of all those saints who lived so well here on earth and are now in heaven; they will not be able to reject me. One could also say: If God throws his cloak around my nakedness, I will be under his protection. But this image is too external. God gives me not only something external but something of himself. I believe this is what grace is: *something of God's own self.*

One could object that a man who had led a life like that of the foreign legionnaire, who certainly had a very bad record, had good reason to ask God to give him something of his own divine self. But what of people who have led a normal life or even (in the case of the saints) an exceptional life, a holy life that went beyond the normal? I believe that the principal difficulty we have with grace today is that many of us—perhaps all of us—feel that we must succeed on our own, we must reach the goal, our life must be in order; we do not like the word "grace" because it reminds us of dependency. Situations of dependency occur all the time in professional life. Many people are dependent on the goodwill of a boss, a politician, or some powerful person; the same may be true of bishops as well! There is something humiliating about the feeling that one could fall out of favor, that one is dependent on the goodwill or displeasure of a superior, on the favor or antipathy of someone else. One is not one's own boss. It is not easy to earn one's wages—even if these are substantial, and one is in no danger of starving—in a situation of dependency. Can one be free if one is dependent on the "grace and favor" of another? And what about our relationship to God? Are we not terribly dependent on him? Does this then mean that grace is something we must beg for? And is this not humiliating? Does it not reduce us to immaturity?

Is grace then incompatible with human dignity? Is it unworthy of the human person to be dependent on grace? This idea lies behind the doctrine of reincarnation, which affirms that one must return to this world again and again. Many people in our society have accepted this teaching and are convinced that one must do everything on one's own: one must work off bit by bit the guilt one incurred through one's mistakes in a previous life. The "consolation" here is that one avoids being dependent on God's favor.

Everything Is Grace

Let us look a little more deeply at the question of the nature of grace. We begin with the sober observation that we are all terribly dependent. There is no human life that is not dependent on other people in a thousand ways, in virtually every sphere. We do indeed possess autonomy, but it is limited. Above all, there is no independence that does not at the same time unambiguously accept the many relationships of dependency. We are dependent on our parents, who gave us our very existence. We are dependent on our environment, on the air we breathe, and on everything that makes life possible. In innumerable contexts, we are dependent on other people.

What would our life be without the many professional services we receive? It would be unlivable. It is not in the least
incompatible with my freedom when I board an aircraft and
am dependent on the pilots, the air traffic controllers, and
many other persons. It is not beneath my dignity to accept
such a high degree of dependency and to need so much help.
Nor does it contradict my independence to be dependent in
my life on the grace and favor of others—"grace" is understood here in a comprehensive sense, covering all the goodwill and friendly assistance we receive from them, and this
includes professional services. I am continuously dependent
on what I receive from others. Self-realization, that great
slogan of our age, is in fact impossible, strictly speaking: to
realize oneself is possible only by means of a huge network of
situations of dependency, the network of what I receive from
others and of the services that we perform for each other.

Tout est grâce, said Saint Thérèse of Lisieux—"Everything
is grace." This is basically true even in the human sphere:
everything is a gift. Paul asks: "What have you that you did
not receive?" (1 Cor 4:7). I can—indeed, I may and must—
affirm this with all my heart. Awareness of this truth is no
sad acknowledgment of our dependency but rather an insight
into the framework that surrounds our freedom. This knowledge does not enslave me. Only a miserable understanding
of human life would claim that I am free only when I need
no one else, when I alone am the lord of my life and need
nothing. Jesus says that he has made himself the servant of all,
and there is no one freer than Jesus. No one affirmed more
resolutely than Jesus his total dependency on the Father. He
does nothing of his own accord. Everything he says and does
is something he has seen with the Father and something the
Father has commissioned him to do. And Jesus is completely
free.

Everything is grace. If this is true even in the human sphere, it is of course particularly true of our relationship to God: "What have you that you did not receive?" A moment's reflection suffices to make it clear that these words of Saint Paul concern the totality of my existence. My life, all my abilities, my understanding, my will, my feelings—all this is God's gift to me. We have received from God the very world in which we live. In short, does anything exist that does not come from God? (The only exception is evil, which does not originate with God; this, however, is not the subject of the present catechesis.)

The obvious question now is this: If all is indeed a gift, what is special about grace? Is there some kind of special favor bestowed by God, going beyond what every human being has anyway in virtue of the fact that he loves, that he lives in this world, that he has various gifts and talents? If all this is already grace, what does it mean to speak as the liturgy does of "baptismal grace" or of the "grace of a vocation"? What is special about grace?

The apostle Paul spoke repeatedly and in unparalleled detail about grace, and the root of what he has to say doubtless lies in the experience of his conversion, when something exceptional happened to him—something that was not simply there all along. When he reflects on his life in his Letter to the Galatians and describes how he came to faith in Christ, he writes: "But when he who had set me apart before I was born, and had called me through his grace, was pleased to reveal his Son to me" (Gal 1:15ff.). It pleased God to call Paul. Paul knows that he did not deserve this in any way—quite the contrary, since he had persecuted Christians and persecuted Christ. On Paul's way to Damascus, Jesus appeared to him and changed his life completely. When we speak of grace, we mean above all this kind of experience, when God intervenes in our life in a special manner. Later, looking back on his conversion and vocation, the apostle writes: "By the grace of God I am what I am, and his grace toward me was not in vain" (1 Cor 15:10). The grace of God has made him what he is: here, therefore, something more is involved than the natural gifts already present in us or the things we can achieve of our own power.

The Characteristics of Grace

The German foreign legionnaire was speaking of something special, something that we have not just taken along as baggage on our journey through life, and he called this "something of God's own self". Grace in the true sense of the word designates a special favor bestowed by God. Let us look at what the *Catechism* says about grace. I shall do so in three steps: First, what does it say about the characteristics of grace? How does one recognize these? Second, what kinds of grace exist? And third, can I experience grace? Can I know how I stand in God's eyes?

We begin with the characteristics of grace. The apostle Paul knew that his vocation was utterly undeserved. I cannot earn grace in the same way that I have a right to my salary at the end of the month or a right to my medical insurance if I have paid my contributions. I have no entitlement to grace. The puzzling thing is that grace is nevertheless necessary: I have no right to it, but I need it. The dying legionnaire knew that without grace, he could not enter heaven. Without this gift, he has no chance at all. But is not this an unjust situation? Does it not remind us afresh of how dependent we are? How are we to understand this apparent contradiction?

For centuries, theologians struggled with this question, and Saint Augustine spent the last years of his life in a bitter struggle to hang on to the affirmation that grace is unmerited. For centuries, the Dominicans and the Jesuits clashed on this question, until one day the pope forbade the discussion. This question tore the West apart. The essential question in the Reformation of Martin Luther was: "How do I find a gracious God?" What about the human contribution? Must I do works in order to move God to be gracious? And how can grace be both unmerited and necessary?

Without pretending to offer a resolution to a debate that has gone on for centuries, I would like to try a very simple approach to this question. Grace means that God freely bestows his favor on the human person, offering him his friendship. God invites us: "Come and share in my life!" Here we may recall the icon of the Holy Trinity by Andrei Rublev (d. 1430). The three angels who visit Abraham sit around a table. In the center of the table, we see a vessel in which a sacrificial animal lies. This icon is a symbolic portrayal of the fellowship of the triune God, of the intimate union of the three divine Persons. The fourth place at table, in the foreground, is empty. That is where we are invited to sit: "Come and receive my friendship!"

This offer is grace. But although friendship is *offered*, it is not automatically present: it is a gift that must first be *received*. It is not present simply in virtue of the fact that God has placed in our heart a yearning to return to our origins or simply because we happen to be pious or religious. This friendship becomes a reality only when we explicitly accept God's invitation as Ananias did when Jesus summoned him and sent him to Saul in Damascus—Ananias said: "Here I am, Lord" (Acts 9:10). Similarly, when God addressed his invitation and his message to Mary, she said: "Let it be to me according to your word" (Lk 1:38). Grace is an offer that needs to be accepted: Are you content to be merely my creature? Do you not also want to be my friend, my child? Do you not want to be my sons and daughters by grace?

This invitation by God can be answered only in freedom; without freedom there is no friendship. And this answer must be made explicitly, when I respond to the offer of grace by accepting it. It is the two elements together that constitute grace—otherwise, as Paul says, grace remains in vain. He can say of himself: "His grace toward me was not in vain", since he had accepted this grace and collaborated with it. He took seriously the offer of friendship. This is a very important element: I have no right to friendship, which is a gift. But friendship with God is vitally necessary, since God created us not only to be his creatures but in order that we might be his children, becoming sons and daughters of God in the Son of God. He created us as free beings so that we could freely accept his offer. Fellowship in the life of God is grace. The Second Letter of Peter speaks of God granting us to "become partakers of the divine nature" (1:4), and the great tradition of the Church says grace deifies the human person by genuinely giving us God's own life.

The Various Forms of Grace

The Church has attempted to analyze the structure of the reality of God's offer to us, so that we can get a better idea of what this deifying grace is. Basically, the Church distinguishes three kinds of grace. First, we have the fundamental offer that God gives us in baptism, the *sanctifying grace* that makes us new persons. Second, we have *actual* or *auxiliary graces* that are offered to us in the various circumstances and situations of our everyday living. Third, we have the so-called *charisms*, special gifts of grace from God that include prophetic gifts, ministerial gifts, and special abilities.

Baptismal Grace

The basis of everything is baptismal grace. The *Catechism* says: "The grace of Christ is the gratuitous gift that God makes to us of his own life, infused by the Holy Spirit into our soul to heal it of sin and to sanctify it. It is the *sanctifying* or *deifying grace* received in Baptism."[1] The text then quotes Saint Paul: "If any one is in Christ, he is a new creation" (2 Cor 5:17). Baptismal grace is truly marvelous! Naturally, if I reflect a little on the momentous words in which the *Catechism* speaks of this baptismal grace, I have to ask: Do other people notice that I am baptized? Do I myself notice it? Saint Gregory Nazianzen, one of the great Fathers of the Church, tells the newly baptized what a glorious gift they have just received: "Baptism is God's most beautiful and magnificent gift.... We call it gift, grace, anointing, enlightenment, garment of immortality, bath of rebirth, seal, and most precious gift."[2]

If then baptism is the most glorious of God's gifts, why do we not notice this more? Why can we not directly sense, see, and perceive the grace of baptism? How can one be sure of the presence of this gift of sanctifying grace? This basic grace of God that we receive in baptism does not belong primarily to the realm of experience but to the realm of faith. I believe that in baptism Christ has taken me into his own life. I believe that my life belongs to Christ. Perhaps I can sense this occasionally, even in the sphere of my emotions; but

[1] *CCC* 1999.
[2] *Oration* 40.3, quoted in *CCC* 1216.

basically, this is something I believe. I believe that in baptism I died and rose again with Christ. I am certain of this in faith, even if I do not feel it. I know that from baptism onward, my life belongs to Christ. This is the reason why we baptize children—not in order to record as many Catholics as possible in the parish registers but because we believe that sanctifying grace is bestowed through baptism. And this means that God takes this human child into his own life, making him a child of God; this means that this child is clothed with Christ and that from now on his life lies in the hands of God.

Nevertheless, the question of experience is not unimportant. Is it possible somehow to perceive grace? I want to know whether God looks on me with favor. How can I experience this?

Actual Graces

We experience actual graces more directly than baptismal grace. The actual or auxiliary graces cover an infinite spectrum: here God is working in my everyday life. Unfortunately, we are so superficial that we fail to perceive many of these graces. But if we look at our lives more closely, we will discover the infinity of little ways in which God helps us, attending to us and responding to our needs. The graces of a conversion, which can turn one's whole life upside down, are large-scale actual graces, but the small graces too are important. For example, when I am praying, a thought or an inspiration occurs to me, and I realize that God is suggesting something to me. Or I feel driven to visit someone and talk to him. Once again, this is the prompting of the Holy Spirit. Before a difficult conversation, I ask God for help and then find that the conversation flows with extraordinary ease; so I thank God for his actual help. Or I miss my bus, but this allows me to have a very important encounter with someone: I see that God stands behind this chain of events. We can experience these kinds of auxiliary graces all the time if we are alert to what is going on in our lives.

These include the graces of one's state in life. How am I to cope with my new task as pastor in a difficult parish, as bishop in a wonderful diocese, or in a new professional situation? Here I experience a special kind of assistance known as the grace of state. There are specific graces for childhood and for old age; there are graces for those who are sick and those who are widowed. But we have to pray for all these graces, which are all expressions of our friendship with God. Paul sees that the more alert he is to receive these graces, the more will his entire life become a cooperation with grace. "I worked harder than any of them," he writes, but adds immediately, "though it was not I, but the grace of God which is with me" (1 Cor 15:10).

Let me say a few words about one actual grace, namely, the grace of forgiveness. This shows us most strongly that God truly gives us his friendship, his own self, something of himself. And perhaps it is precisely the experiences of forgiveness that allow us to *see* that God truly looks on us with favor.

Charisms

There is an immense variety of charisms, the special gifts of grace, but they all share one characteristic: they are given to me, not for my own self, but for others. If I receive the charism of preaching, this is not bestowed for my own private enjoyment but is meant to be useful to the Church. If I receive the charism of prophecy, this is not for myself but for others. Charisms do not make one holier. The fact that

someone has received the gift of miraculous healings does
not make him a saint: it is for others that he has been given
this charism. Similarly, the episcopal and priestly ministries
are charisms, gifts that one receives, not for oneself, but for
others.[3]

Can I Be Certain?

God gives me something of his own self: that is what grace
is. But can I be certain of this? Can one experience it?
The *Catechism* says very clearly and categorically: "Since it
belongs to the supernatural order, grace *escapes our experience*
and cannot be known except by faith."[4] Do I know whether
my life is pleasing to God? Can I be certain that I am in his
grace? Well, I am not saying this with the aim of making you
uneasy, but the *Catechism* continues: "We cannot therefore
rely on our feelings or our works."[5] No matter how much
I may have done, I am not certain that I am pleasing to
God. But the text then affirms: "However, according to the
Lord's words—'Thus you will know them by their fruits'
[Mt 7:20]—reflection on God's blessings in our life and in
the lives of the saints offers us a guarantee that grace is at
work in us." The fruits show us that grace is at work in us,
and this encourages us to believe ever more strongly and to
adopt an attitude of trustful poverty. "I stand before God
with empty hands," said Saint Thérèse of Lisieux, "and I do
not ask you to count my works but to clothe me with your
righteousness."

[3] On this, see *CCC* 799–801.
[4] *CCC* 2005.
[5] Ibid., cf. Council of Trent, Denzinger-Schönmetzer, *Enchiridion Symbolorum, definitionum et declarationum de rebus fidei et morum* (1965), 1533–1534.

I should like to conclude with some marvelous words of another saint, Joan of Arc, the Maid of Orléans, who was twenty-one years old when she was brought to trial before judges who were the great theologians of those days. They put all kinds of tricky questions to this illiterate girl, including the question of whether she was certain that she was in grace. Joan of Arc gave a wonderful reply that we all could use as a prayer: *Si je n'y suis que Dieu m'y mette; si j'y suis que Dieu m'y garde*—"If I am not in grace, may God put me there; if I am in grace, may God keep me there." This young woman expressed quite wonderfully the trust with which we should hope in God's grace—on which we most certainly may count.

"JUSTIFIED BY GOD"

The Vocation to Holiness

Accompany us on our earthly pilgrimage toward the blessed homeland, where we hope to arrive in order to contemplate forever the glory of the Father, the Son, and the Holy Spirit. Amen.

—Prayer of Pope John Paul II
Canonization of Saint Pio of Pietrelcina,
June 16, 2002

A New Saint

It is fascinating to see how popular today is Padre Pio—the holy Capuchin priest from Pietrelcina who spent most of his life in the little monastery of San Giovanni Rotondo near Foggia. More pilgrims travel to his tomb than to Lourdes; their number is estimated at seven million a year. Everywhere in Italy, and indeed throughout the world, we find a great love for Padre Pio. The question of justification—being "justified" by God (Rom 8:30)—and the vocation to holiness take on a special visibility in this saint, and this is why I am particularly happy to speak about him, to join with the hundreds of thousands who traveled to his canonization and the many millions who venerate the new saint.

I myself had the happiness of seeing Padre Pio in 1961, when my home parish went on pilgrimage. I was sixteen years old at that time and had a rather critical attitude toward all these phenomena. At sixteen, I was somewhat reserved when I saw the enthusiastic southern Italian women quarreling at the church door about which of them was to get the front seat, and then disregarding every form of love of neighbor as they stormed into the church; or when I saw the many devotional objects on sale in the precincts of the monastery even at that date—Padre Pio with snow, Padre Pio on a thermometer, Padre Pio everywhere.

We went to the church very early in the morning, and I do not think I have ever again experienced a Mass like that or seen a priest celebrate the way Padre Pio did that one time I was privileged to be present. The way in which this simple Capuchin priest celebrated the Mass made an unforgettable impression on many people. When one saw him at the offertory (the presentation of the gifts), at the consecration, or at communion, one sensed: What is happening here is absolutely real. This is not a rite in which someone is participating externally; this is *the event*. That which the sacrament signifies is taking place, namely, the sacrifice of Christ, in which Padre Pio shared in his own body in the stigmata and which he made so clearly visible when he celebrated Mass.

I could not go to confession to him, since one had to speak Italian and I did not yet know that language; but I have heard the stories of many who did confess their sins to him. There too his attentiveness and his humor were incomparable, but his severity was inexorable when conversion and repentance were at stake. As soon as he sensed even the tiniest trace of repentance, his mercy knew no bounds.

For fifty years he bore the stigmata of Christ on his body. He died in 1968, two days after the fiftieth anniversary of the day on which he had received the wounds of Christ. This was certainly one reason why hordes of curious people streamed to San Giovanni Rotondo, but there was another reason too: the encounter with the love of Christ, which moved people profoundly, inspired them, and set in motion a conversion in their lives.

Another reason was his intense love for the poor and the little ones. He used the copious donations that he received to build the Home for the Relief of Suffering, a magnificent hospital, one of the best in Italy, with outstanding doctors; this is still being extended today. He wanted the poor to be treated there as Christ himself would treat them, with the greatest kindness and the best medical care.

Many people experienced signs of his presence. They experienced the closeness of heaven and the saints in extraordinary phenomena that have been attested to again and again—for example, the fragrance that announced his presence; his apparitions; his bilocations (many people have borne witness that he was simultaneously present in more than one place); but above all, the innumerable experiences of concrete, simple, daily help from heaven. All this moves us to great joy and thankfulness that God gives us signs of his closeness even today.

"Justified before God"

Let us now turn to the doctrine of our faith: What is *holiness*? First, however, we must ask: What is *justification*, which precedes holiness and without which holiness is impossible? Justification and holiness are closely linked. We are all called to be holy before God, because God himself is holy; but we can do so only if we are justified before God, in other words, when we can pass the examination before the face of God. This is certainly a dramatic question: Can we, can our life, stand up to examination by God? Let us recall the story Jesus tells in the Gospel about the Pharisee and the tax collector. The Pharisee prays full of gratitude for all the good things he does, for the piety in his life, and for the fact that he is not like the tax collector. The latter does not even dare to raise his eyes to heaven and asks only that God may be merciful to him, a poor sinner. Jesus comments: "I tell you, this man went down to his house justified rather than the other" (Lk 18:9–14). What does "justified" mean? What does it mean to stand before God in such a way that we can pass the examination in his presence?

In his Letter to the Romans, Paul writes: "Since, therefore, we are now justified by his blood, much more shall we be saved by him from the wrath of God" (5:9). Christ's blood has made us just, so that we can survive under God's judgment. What does this mean?

An Indian Jesuit, Father Anthony de Mello, wrote many books that found a wide readership. In one of them, he tells a story:

Believing that God had appeared to her, a woman went to the bishop to ask for his advice. The bishop said to her: "You may believe in apparitions, but I would ask you to accept that it is I, as bishop of the diocese, who decide whether your apparitions are genuine or false."

The woman replied, "Certainly, Your Excellency."

"So you will do what I require of you?"

"Certainly, Your Excellency."

"Good; then listen carefully. You say that God has appeared to you. Next time he appears, you will carry out an experiment, and then I will know if it is really God."

"Very well, Your Excellency. But what kind of experiment do you have in mind?"

"Tell God: 'Please reveal to me the personal and private sins of the bishop!' If it is really God who is appearing to you, he will reveal my sins to you. Then come back and tell me everything—but don't tell anyone else. Okay?"

"I will do as Your Excellency says."

One month later, the woman asked for another appointment with the bishop, who questioned her: "Did God appear to you again?"

"I believe so, Your Excellency."

"And did you ask him the question I told you to ask?"

"Certainly, Your Excellency."

"And what did God say?"

"God told me: 'Go to the bishop and tell him that I have forgotten all his sins.' "

I liked this story immediately. It would be lovely if God had simply forgotten all my sins! But as I reflected on it in preparation for this catechesis, I began to have my doubts. Something tells me that God could not really have said that to the woman. If I were the bishop in the story, would I have been convinced that God had spoken to her? I do not think this would be the case. Indeed, I hope this would not be the case! Has God forgotten my sins? If so, this may be good, but does it help me? After all, I have not forgotten them! It may be nice for me to think that God has forgotten my sins; but what about my conscience? No; I do not think it is desirable that God should forget my sins but rather that he should forgive them. If he forgot them, they would no longer exist in his memory—but they would still exist in mine! I would look good in God's eyes, but nothing would have changed

when I looked at myself. Naturally, I do not want to rule out
the possibility that Anthony de Mello told this story simply
to make the same point as King Hezekiah, when he prays:
"You have cast all my sins behind your back" (Is 38:17). In
other words, God no longer looks at our sins. But I believe
that something important is lacking here.

As I reflected on this catechesis, I found a passage from
the Letter to the Romans very helpful. I have already quoted
from it; I believe that it says something deeper than just that
God forgets my sins:

> While we were yet helpless, at the right time Christ died for
> the ungodly. Why, one will hardly die for a righteous man—
> though perhaps for a good man one will dare even to die. But
> God shows his love for us in that while we were yet sinners
> Christ died for us. Since, therefore, we are now justified by
> his blood, much more shall we be saved by him from the
> wrath of God. For if while we were still enemies we were
> reconciled to God *by the death of his Son*, much more, now
> that we are reconciled, shall we be *saved by his life*. Not only
> so, but we also rejoice in God through our Lord Jesus Christ,
> through whom we have now received our reconciliation.
> (Rom 5:6–11; emphasis added)

This is different from Anthony de Mello's story. I do not wish
to take up the old controversy about the doctrine of justification here; this has separated Catholics and Protestants since the
sixteenth century and led to bitter theological debates. I should
simply like to ask: What does "justification by the blood of
Christ" mean? I believe that this does not mean that God has
merely forgotten our guilt or only acquitted us (as was said
over and over again in the controversy between Protestants
and Catholics). It is of course true that he has acquitted us,
but the decisive point is surely that he has reconciled us, in
other words, that our situation has changed. He has not merely

forgotten the burden of sin that we bear on our shoulders: he has removed this burden from us. He has truly reconciled us and given us new life, without any merit on our part, "while we were still enemies". This is a pure work of grace, nothing that we deserved.

It is here that the Christian faith brings something new. It was already prepared in the Old Testament and then fully revealed in Christ. We often hear, doubtless not wholly incorrectly, that the non-Christian religions show various ways by which we can approach God (or the divine sphere). Often, the gods, the god, the divine sphere can be brought to look on human beings with favor, or can be appeased, through cultic actions, sacrifice, prayer, or penance. Our acts of sin have enraged the divine sphere, and we must undertake considerable labors in order to reconcile ourselves with it.

This understanding already existed at the time of the Bible, but the biblical view is a paradoxical reverse of this: it is not we who do something in order to reconcile God to ourselves, but it is God who incomprehensibly acts in order to reconcile us to himself. He takes the initiative in full freedom. In total and sovereign autonomy, he acts to bring us back to himself. He tears down the wall that separates us from him and reconciles us to himself.

The Letter to the Romans is the apostle Paul's great text on the subject of reconciliation. Here we read:

> For there is no distinction; since all [i.e., both Jews and Gentiles] have sinned and fall short of the glory of God, they are justified by his grace as a gift, through the redemption which is in Christ Jesus, whom God put forward as an expiation by his blood, to be received by faith. (Rom 3:22–25)

A literal translation of these words would be: "God made him the instrument of expiation, which we can take hold of by faith."

It is not we who must display to God works of reconciliation. God does not simply bestow on us the forgiveness of sins, nor does he forget these. He forgives us our sins by placing in our hands an instrument that allows us to enter into fellowship with him. And this instrument, which we are permitted to lay hold of in faith, is the blood of Jesus Christ. Paul continues:

> This was to show God's righteousness, because in his divine forbearance he had passed over former sins; it was to prove at the present time that he himself is righteous and that he justifies him who has faith in Jesus. (Rom 3:25–26)

He is righteous, and he makes righteous. He makes us righteous when we lay hold of Jesus Christ in faith.

Justification Makes the Human Person New

God reconciles us to himself. It is he who brings about expiation. This is a total reversal of perspective: it is not our labors that appease God but his prevenient love (i.e., the love that "comes to meet us") that creates us anew. Let us now see how this takes place. The first step of prevenient grace in our life is baptism. We can say that baptism is possible only because God took the first step toward us by sending his Son for the whole world. In baptism, all this becomes a reality in *my* life.

Bishops seldom have occasion to baptize children. Each time it is a great joy for me to know in faith what is happening in the sacrament. Padre Pio too took great pleasure in baptizing children and often did so. Clearly, he was aware on a deeper level than most of us of what happens in baptism. Prevenient grace is implanted in a human life and establishes a positive direction for the whole of that life. And this is why the Catholic Church is decisively in favor of infant baptism: baptism is always prevenient grace and we are always its recipients, whether aware or unaware, whether we are already adults and can say our Yes to the sacrament in faith, or our parents and godparents must do this for us. Grace always comes to meet us and brings us into the sphere of a new life where we are fully accepted.

It is precisely infant baptism that shows us how much grace is a prevenient gift, God's pure act of justification, not a response to any action of ours. And this prevenient grace aims at awakening our collaboration: when God justifies us in the grace of baptism through Jesus Christ, through his blood, he addresses an appeal to our whole life, urging us to respond to this grace. And the repentance with which we must respond to this grace is a lifelong task. It is not enough to say: "I converted when I was fifteen or eighteen or twenty-seven, and since then everything has been fine."

The *Catechism* teaches: "The first work of the grace of the Holy Spirit is *conversion*, effecting justification in accordance with Jesus' proclamation at the beginning of the Gospel: 'Repent, for the kingdom of heaven is at hand' [Mt 4:17]. Moved by grace, man turns towards God and away from sin."[1] Justification begins as God's prevenient gift, which summons us to respond. The Council of Trent (1545–1563) replied to the challenge of the Reformation by affirming that justification means not only that my sins are forgiven but also that my inner self is sanctified and renewed.[2] Thanks to justification, sin is no longer counted against me, and an inner transformation takes place. The *Catechism* continues: "Justification *detaches man from sin* which contradicts the love of God, and purifies his heart of sin. Justification follows upon God's merciful initiative of

---

[1] *CCC* 1989.
[2] Decree on Justification, chap. 7; *CCC* 1989.

offering forgiveness. It reconciles man with God. It frees from the enslavement to sin, and it heals."[3]

"Justification is at the same time *the acceptance of God's righteousness* through faith in Jesus Christ. Righteousness (or 'justice') here means the rectitude of divine love."[4] The entire dynamic of this event demands that we respond in love to the love bestowed on us. And this is why justification always means an invitation to collaborate with God. A synergy (to use the modern economic term) is meant to take place, the collaboration between God's grace and human freedom. And once we start to cooperate with grace, we discover that this very act of collaboration with the grace of God is itself a gift. When I put into practice the promptings of the Holy Spirit, when I respond to God's love, I know that this answer of mine is itself a gift—a gift given to me in order that I in turn may give it. This is why the Council of Trent says:

> When God touches the human heart by the enlightenment of the Holy Spirit, the human person does not remain completely inactive, since he accepts an inspiration which he could in fact also have rejected; on the other hand, he cannot raise himself of his own free will to the status of righteousness before God. For this, he requires the grace of God.[5]

In the preface at Mass on the feast day of a saint, we pray: "In crowning their merits, you crown your own gifts." The saints bear witness that their whole response in love to the love of God was his gift to them. Nevertheless, it is a genuine collaboration.

Saint Augustine once made an extraordinary affirmation, which almost seems exaggerated: "The justification of the

[3] *CCC* 1990.
[4] *CCC* 1991.
[5] Decree on Justification, chap. 5.

godless is a greater work than the creation of heaven and earth." He explains this as follows: "Heaven and earth will pass away, but the salvation and the justification of the elect will abide for ever."[6] The miracle of conversion is greater than the creation of heaven and earth. We find a similar affirmation in Saint Paul: "For it is the God who said, 'Let light shine out of darkness,' who has shone in our hearts to give the light of the knowledge of the glory of God in the face of Christ" (2 Cor 4:6). In other words, the God who made the world has done an even greater work. The grace of justification accomplishes something greater than would happen if God were to forget our sins: it makes the inner person new, a genuinely new creature. Through the grace of conversion— even if this is never definitively and perfectly grasped as long as we are en route here on earth—we are permitted to *experience* the fact that there is no greater joy than to convert to the living God. This is the miracle of justification.

What Is Holiness?

This brings us to the question: What makes people holy? We may summarize by saying that holiness means nothing other than reaching the goal of our life. We pray to God for one another in order that we may reach the goal of our life. At the end of this series of catecheses on the foundations of Christian morality, let us once again ask what the goal of our life is—for the point of morality is to orient us to this goal. The words of the apostle Peter show us the path:

> Gird up your minds, be sober, set your hope fully upon the grace that is coming to you at the revelation of Jesus Christ.

[6] *Commentary on the Gospel of John* 72.3.

As obedient children, do not be conformed to the passions of
your former ignorance, but as he who called you is holy, be
holy yourselves in all your conduct; since it is written, "You
shall be holy, for I am holy." (1 Pet 1:13–16)

Let me first ask about the essence of this holiness and then
see whether it is possible for us to take this path. I will then
indicate four paths that take us toward this goal.

Holiness is nothing other than the realization of the goal
of our life. We read on the first page of the Bible that God
made us in his own image and likeness (Gen 1:26). To the
extent that we come to resemble this image, we attain the
goal of our life. A saint is one who has realized the image
of God that he bears in himself. This image was developed,
so to speak, until it reached full likeness to its origin. The
saint is a living image of God. In concrete terms, this means
becoming like Christ, for it is he who is the perfect image of
God. Blessed Raymond of Capua (d. 1399), general of the
Dominican order and father confessor of Saint Catherine of
Siena, relates that her face was transformed when she con-
fessed her sins so that he saw Christ in her. I believe that this
is the secret of holiness.

Paul writes in the Letter to the Romans:

We know that in everything God works for good with those
who love him.... For those whom he foreknew he also predestined to be conformed to the image of his Son, in order
that he might be the first-born among many brethren. And
those whom he predestined he also called; and those whom
he called he also justified; and those whom he justified he also
glorified. (8:28–30)

We have all received this vocation. When God creates us in
his own image, he also calls us to realize this image. Is this
possible? In the archdiocesan library, we have a monumental

work, the *Acta Sanctorum*. Industrious Jesuits in the seven-teenth century began to collect all available information about the lives of the saints, and about thirty thick folio vol-umes were compiled in the course of three or four centuries. If you open these books, you will find an immense number of saints listed under each day of the year; a small selection of these saints is included in the so-called *Roman Martyrology*, which the pope recently published. In the *Martyrology*, for example, we find thirteen saints under today's date, June 16, but this is only a small selection: in the *Acta Sanctorum*, thirty-nine saints are listed individually, and a group of 404 martyrs from Gaul is commemorated on this date. And these in turn are only those persons who have been officially canonized or who are attested in the Acts of the Martyrs.

There can be no doubt that the twentieth century saw a greater number of martyrs than any other period in Chris-tian history. The Holy Father asked a few years ago that a list of these modern martyrs be compiled, and about twenty thousand biographies have been collected of persons who laid down their lives for the sake of their faith in the twentieth century. They will never all be canonized; there are simply too many of them for that. But they are certainly saints in the sight of God, and persons whom we can venerate for their holiness. And the total number of saints is even greater. Only God knows the number of those who are great in heaven. Clearly, it is possible to become a saint!

If then it is possible, what path leads to holiness? Thanks to the Internet, I have been able to read the sermon that the Holy Father [John Paul II] preached this morning in Rome at the canonization of Padre Pio. The pope mentions four elements, and I believe that these have a universal validity, although of course they must be lived differently in keeping with each individual's way of life.

Take His Yoke Upon You

First: "*Take my yoke upon you* and learn from me.... For my yoke is easy, and my burden is light" (Mt 11:29–30; emphasis added). The Holy Father begins with these words from the Gospels and says that Padre Pio shows that Jesus is indeed *dolce*, "sweet, mild, light". Padre Pio's life bears witness to this. Compared with so many other things that people take on their shoulders, the yoke of Jesus is light. And the pope goes on to say that this yoke is the cross of Jesus. Padre Pio sought and realized in his life an ever-greater configuration to the crucified Lord, not out of love for suffering, but in order to share in the redemptive work of Jesus Christ.

This was his motivation; this was his passion. He lived and suffered in order to give people the grace of Christ. In God's plan, the cross is the true instrument of salvation for all persons. It is the way that Jesus explicitly proposes for those who follow him. The pope says that it is only on this path of self-denial and the cross that we can come to resemble Christ. (And if one looks at the pope, one will see how seriously he himself takes this path.)

The Mercy of God

The second characteristic of Padre Pio is certainly valid for all who seek the path of holiness: he showed forth *the mercy of God*. One of the great characteristics of holiness in the twentieth century was the fact that the mercy of God was proclaimed and experienced in a way hitherto unparalleled. The central figures here are Saint Thérèse of Lisieux, who died at the very end of the nineteenth century; Saint Faustina (d. 1938); and most especially Padre Pio. The boundlessness of the divine compassion in the saints has its source in their configuration to the cross of Christ: the closer Padre Pio drew to the crucified Christ, the greater was his compassion.

I could relate many anecdotes to illustrate this boundless compassion in the life of Padre Pio. One felt this above all when he offered the sacrifice of the Mass for the whole world. When he lifted up the paten at the offertory (the presentation of the gifts), this action often took a long time. We knew that he was interceding for many people so that they might receive the mercy of God. His compassion was also seen in the confessional.

Naturally, Padre Pio could also be very strict. Someone once told me that he himself had seen how Padre Pio suddenly turned around during the Mass, which he was celebrating *ad orientem*. He scanned the church, looking for someone, and then cried out: *Via! Via!* ("Get out! Get out!"). The man whom he had addressed slunk out of the church, red with shame. Padre Pio pointed his finger at him and did not turn back to the altar until the man had in fact left. Clearly, Padre Pio knew in his heart that this man needed to be prodded and shaken before he would repent. And as a matter of fact, the man went to confession to the saint three days later. This is mercy, an ardent desire for other people's salvation, for conversion, a passion to spread God's love for the world.

Prayer

Third, the Holy Father says that the deepest reason for the apostolic success of Padre Pio was his *intimate union with God in prayer*, in long hours of prayer. He used to say: *Io sono un povero frate, chi prega* ("I am a poor brother who prays"). The Holy Father calls prayer our best weapon, a key to open the heart of God.

Works of Charity

The fourth element that the Holy Father mentions is the link between prayer and active works of charity, which was always present in Padre Pio. His passionate love for the poor, the little ones, and the suffering took concrete form in the great hospital in San Giovanni Rotondo. The pope says that prayer and love of neighbor form the synthesis of Padre Pio's life in holiness.

Here we have the four steps toward holiness that the Holy Father enumerated in Saint Peter's Square this morning: taking up the cross in imitation of Christ; compassion; prayer; and love of neighbor. I close with the prayer with which he ended his homily this morning:

> "I bless you, Father, Lord of heaven and earth, because ... these things ... you have revealed to little ones" (Mt 11:25). How appropriate are these words of Jesus, when we think of them as applied to you, humble and beloved Padre Pio. Teach us, we ask you, humility of heart so we may be counted among the little ones of the Gospel, to whom the Father promised to reveal the mysteries of his Kingdom. Help us to pray without ceasing, certain that God knows what we need even before we ask him. Obtain for us the eyes of faith that will be able to recognize right away in the poor and suffering the face of Jesus. Sustain us in the hour of the combat and of the trial and, if we fall, make us experience the joy of the sacrament of forgiveness. Grant us your tender devotion to Mary, the Mother of Jesus and our Mother. Accompany us on our earthly pilgrimage toward the blessed homeland, where we hope to arrive in order to contemplate forever the glory of the Father, the Son and the Holy Spirit. Amen.[7]

---

[7] John Paul II, June 16, 2002, Holy See website, www.vatican.va.